ANTHOLOGY
OF
CLASSIC
ARTICLES III

ANTHOLOGY
OF
CLASSIC
ARTICLES III

The Christian Science Publishing Society
210 Massachusetts Avenue, Boston, Massachusetts 02115 USA

Anthology of Classic Articles III

ISBN: 978-0-87510-488-1
G750B51411EN

PUR1203007.5

Printed in USA

TABLE OF CONTENTS

INTRODUCTION

⟨~⟩

*M*any readers love having a collection of classic articles that they can turn to easily—and they've asked for more! So, here we offer the *Anthology of Classic Articles III*—a carefully composed selection of previously published articles. Some of the selections may be new to you, others treasured friends, but you're sure to find them fresh with inspiration and deep meaning for today.

The articles in this compilation are drawn from issues from the first 126 years of *The Christian Science Journal* and 107 years of the *Christian Science Sentinel*. These articles have been enthusiastically recommended by a group of Christian Science practitioners and teachers as being particularly helpful in their healing work. This, like any anthology, gathers an array of well-loved, dog-eared, and scribbled-on pages from far-flung personal libraries into one freshly-printed, convenient book—with a goal of increasing readers' inspiration and healing acumen.

Mary Baker Eddy, the Discoverer and Founder of Christian Science, began publishing the monthly *Journal* in 1883, and the weekly *Sentinel* in 1898, to spread the news that the healing principles taught by Christ Jesus were still in effect, and once again actively healing "all manner of sickness and all manner of disease among the people" (Matthew 4:23). Those magazines are still being published today, as the record of spiritual healing as practiced by Christian Scientists continues to grow.

In the back of this collection you'll find indexes of subjects, authors, and publication dates, as well as more information about Mary Baker Eddy and her book *Science and Health with Key to the Scriptures*. To subscribe to current issues of *The Christian Science Journal* and the *Christian Science Sentinel*, or to purchase a copy of *Science and Health*, please visit a local Christian Science Reading Room or *www.christianscience.com/shop*.

The Christian Science Publishing Society

ADJUSTING MEMORY'S MECHANISM

*T*here are many things mortals need to remember and others they prefer to forget. If memory's mechanism seems maladjusted and a human being cannot recall what he should remember, or if he is plagued with the recurrence of unhappy thought pictures of past events, this condition can be healed through prayer. There is a law of God that will heal amnesia, remove a mental block, and restore memory, or else enable one to bring under control thoughts that one feels would be better forgotten—whichever adjustment a case may seem to need.

The divine Mind is omniscient. This Mind holds safely within itself its own ideas. Not one true thought is ever lost or even temporarily forgotten. Omniactive, omnipresent, omnipotent Mind is always intelligent. Thoughts are continually unfolding in this Mind in orderly sequence. Mind is never absent, but is invariably present, alert, strong, and true. No haziness or dreaminess obscures the clarity of Mind's consciousness of its ideas. They are sharply defined, each with its own purpose and importance, held in the divine memory by indissoluble bands of love and vividly discerned.

Since man is the manifestation of immortal Mind, he is endowed with the faculty of infallible memory. This faculty can never be lost or become dim, and is never ill at ease, plagued by unhappy recollections. Mary Baker Eddy writes in *Science and Health with Key to the Scriptures:* "If delusion says, 'I have lost my memory,' contradict it. No faculty of Mind is lost. In Science, all being is eternal, spiritual, perfect, harmonious in every action" (*Science and Health,* p. 407).

One who grasps the beauty and grandeur of God's creation will always love to remember. He will have no problem in holding in conscious thought the ideas he has previously received from Mind. They will be etched in consciousness as with "the point of a diamond" (Jer. 17:1).

Memory is a precious gift from God, Mind, to man. From Mind, divine Love, emanate thoughts of love, which in their turn produce harmonious events, beautiful experiences, happy memories. No trivial or ignoble thoughts proceed from so grand a source as Love, omnipotent Principle, to hover accusingly in consciousness and remind one of wasted opportunities and misspent effort. Mind, Truth, holds no bitterness, no sadness, no regrets. All that truly exists or occurs in true consciousness is grand. It is worthy of remembrance and can never be lost.

Whatever in human thought is discordant, disturbing, of unhappy memory, does not emanate from divine Mind; therefore it is not true or permanent but as ephemeral as a dream—and as easily forgotten by one who is willing to admit its unreality and let it go. Mrs. Eddy writes: "Whatever obstructs the way,—causing to stumble, fall, or faint, those mortals who are striving to enter the path,—divine Love will remove; and uplift the fallen and strengthen the weak. Therefore, give up thy earth-weights; and observe the apostle's admonition, 'Forgetting those things which are behind, and reaching forth unto those which are before'" (*Miscellaneous Writings,* p. 328).

Christian Science shows, then, that the understanding of divine Love can adjust the mechanism of human memory—whether it is operating sluggishly, forgetting when it should recall, or too imaginatively, bringing to consciousness images of mortal thought better forgotten. These thoughts have in truth no more substance than dreams and should be allowed to fall into the oblivion from which they came. Christ Jesus said, "Let the dead bury their dead" (Matt. 8:22). Human will is often inadequate to bring about this burial—to unclasp the hold of mortal mind on its own false images. But the recognition of God, Love, as the only Mind and creator enables one to classify the ugliness of the past as a shadow and then to consign it to oblivion as one who has awakened from sleep drops the memory of a dream when he recognizes its unreality.

Since the divine Mind is omniscient and man reflects the qualities of Mind, the age of a human being is no argument for a loss of memory. Memory is immortal, not subject to the brain. Matter does not make conditions for spiritual ideas, nor time impose a penalty. Mind is infinite. Its capacity has no limits. All that exists in Truth is eternally in divine consciousness and forever present. Every individual man and woman reflects the capacity of the omnipresent, creative Mind. Each can claim the capability to know all that he requires to know at the moment he needs the knowledge.

Memory improves in human experience in proportion as the individual claims and cherishes the immortal faculty that Christian Science is showing he possesses by divine right. Perfect memory is a spiritual bestowal to be valued and utilized. A person who treats carelessly such a precious gift may lose his conscious grasp of it and become forgetful, absentminded, senile.

It is never too late to have a lost memory restored—to prove that Mind is ever present and memory always clear—for in Truth it is never lost. Man is eternally at one with omnipotent Mind, and manifests its qualities forever. Knowing this, the wise children of this world claim and utilize to the utmost the mental faculties they truly derive from God. They love to remember because they recognize all true objects and events to be the manifestation of divine Love. They exercise and will develop their God-derived faculty for remembering, and aim to demonstrate the infinitude of immortal memory.

—*Naomi Price*

"As thyself"

So often I had proudly said,
    "I love my neighbor,"
(remembering the healing thoughts I'd fed
    to friends in need,
the honor shown to parents,
the kindness shown to strangers,
the unselfed sacrifices in my day).

But this was not enough,
and in its quiet, heartfelt way
the Christly message came:
"Thou shalt love thy neighbour *as thyself*."

Then I saw how incomplete
the circle of my love had been—
I'd felt no love for me.
Self-condemnation, doubt, inadequacy,
criticism's barb and fear's debris
had bound my thought.

"Thou shalt love thy neighbour *as thyself*."
So I began to feed myself
    constructive thoughts,
such as confidence, compassion,
    and support—
truths all-powerful to thwart
    destructive sense,
the error that would try
    to crucify the Christ in me.

I learned how to pray—
protect my thought—
to assure myself each day,
"Beloved, you are God's own,
completely free from sin."
And as Love purified my sense of self,
I felt a warmth and joy within,
and a freedom I had never known.
Self-condemnation was dethroned.

Then I knew I loved my neighbor
even better than before,
for now I loved him as myself
and loved myself much more.

—*Sandra Luerssen Hoerner*

BELIEFS CANNOT FASTEN ON MAN

*B*arnacles have in the past fastened themselves in great numbers to the hulls of ocean-going ships and, if they have not from time to time been removed, they have considerably retarded the ships' movements. Chemical research has now provided a paint for ships' hulls which, by its chemical properties, prevents barnacles from fastening themselves to the bottoms of the ships.

Many mortals are unhappy because they believe that some form of sin, sickness, impairment, unpleasant relationship, or untoward circumstance has fastened itself barnacle-like on their lives, and they see no way to gain their freedom. They believe that evil can fasten and attach itself to them in some form, and that they have little hope of successfully disputing its aggressive claim. If what mortals see, hear, and feel materially is accepted as final evidence of the condition of man, this sad conclusion is justified.

Christian Science, however, is awakening thought to discover a better and truer sense of existence, the spiritual sense. This concept of being shows God, the one cause, to be boundless Spirit, Mind, the source and substance of all that really is, and man, individually and collectively, to be the evidence, or expression, of God; therefore Mind-like and spiritual, not mortal and matter-like.

Radical as this teaching is in its unqualified denial of the substantiality of matter, and in its assertion of the unreliability of material sense testimony, it is gaining the respect and adherence of thinkers who find no hope for enduring health, happiness, peace, and continuing progress on any but a spiritual basis—the infinitude of Mind, constituting, containing, and conditioning all identities.

This concept of Life and its representative, man, Christ Jesus taught and demonstrated. He said that as we know or understand what is spiritually true, we find our freedom from all that is afflictive and untrue. He said nothing about evil being able to fasten its conditions on us, but he showed that a clear apprehension of the spiritual idea of God and man demonstrates man's continuous superiority to evil's claim that it can fasten forms of discord on him. His healing works graphically illustrate this.

Daily let us realize and declare that our individuality is not what the material mind says it is—a composite of cells and chemicals subject to enigmatical forces of chance and circumstance—and see that this is but the misconception of man, whose being is really eternal Mind's representative and idea, spiritual, harmonious, and Godlike. As we begin to realize this, we see how we can prove that no sin, disease, or discord can ever fasten itself to our manhood. We see that the only "I" or "Us" is God, in whom all true individuality eternally is. Shadows cannot fasten themselves to sunbeams. No more can the ignorant, darkish beliefs and conditions of evil attach themselves to your individuality or to mine, forever living in and by God.

Apropos of this is the following statement by Mary Baker Eddy: "Evil seeks to fasten all error upon God, and so make the lie seem part of eternal Truth" (*Unity of Good*, p. 17). God as Life is evidenced only by the identities manifesting this Life; so evil, seeking, as it seems to human sense, to fasten all error on God, seeks to fasten it on God's manifestation, on man, beast, flower, shrub, tree, whose only true identity is in and of God.

Science reveals the impossibility of suppositional mortal mind, the basic error, ever reaching beyond its own realm of supposition. It has no leverage by which to lift itself above its own dead level, no power by which it can project its lies of sin, sickness, impairment, and discord out of its fictional realm into infinite Mind, there to fasten them on God's ideas.

The student of Christian Science, realizing something of man's God-given spiritual individuality, is able to prove in daily experience for himself and others that man's identity is never in the clutches of evil. Evil has nothing with which to fasten its negativeness to the positive substance that is God, Mind, individualized in man.

What is mindless cannot affix itself to Mind; what is evil cannot fasten itself on good; what is error cannot annex itself to Truth; what is matter cannot join itself to Spirit. The Christian Scientist knows that there is nothing in God's image and expression to which evil can attach itself. God and every one of His ideas are forever safe and secure. The evil and suppositional can never even touch, let alone fasten themselves to, the good and the actual.

When Paul was shipwrecked on the island of Melita, we are told that after he had built a fire "there came a viper out of the heat, and fastened on his hand. ... And he shook off the beast into the fire, and felt no harm" (Acts 28:3, 5). Paul must have known that evil cannot fasten any error upon God. Therefore it cannot fasten any of its lies, including a poison-exuding reptile, on the identity of God's expression, man.

A poisonous beast fastening itself to a mortal's physical body is but one form of animated error attaching itself to another. The scene is in the suppositional realm of mortal mind, a realm in which God's man never appears. He remains forever in his perpetual oneness with God, the All-in-all, never disengaged from omnipresent good, and eternally superior to error's claim that it can fasten its lies on God and His son.

In the degree these truths are understood, men find their freedom from, and dominion over, the false phenomena called sins, diseases, and other forms of affliction which evil says it can fasten on God and His man. Against evil's lying claim, man is fully protected by the Christ, the spiritual idea of God and man.

—Paul Stark Seeley

CHANGE OF HEART

The heart of Love is always strong and sound;
God knows no other heart.
Forever equal to the hour's demand,
it can sustain no shock, can take no hurt.

The heart of Love is warm and deeply tender,
not hard or cold or cruel;
no weary disillusion dims the splendor
that lights the shining heart of all things real.

The heart of Love is never breached or broken;
at ease, at peace, at one,
alone, but never lonely or forsaken,
the heart of Love is satisfied with man.

The false, material, personal sense of heart,
as dust to dust, withdraws.
Healed and released, we see the lie depart
with all its empty griefs, its shadowy joys.

There are not many hearts, but one heart only—
quick, eager, glad, alive,
forever acting strongly and serenely,
inviolate, single, whole—the heart of Love.

—Peter J. Henniker-Heaton

THE CHRIST-EXAMPLE: REFLECTION AND HEALING

In searching for an understanding of our true identity, we soon learn in Christian Science that man is in reality God's reflection. But what does this mean to us? We find the answers richly illumined in Christ Jesus' words and example.

Jesus had a divinely pure sense of his relation to the Father, and he held to it constantly. His sublime Christian metaphysics makes crystal-clear what it means to say that man is God's reflection. With divine insight he affirmed this spiritual relationship in terms that captured the absolute truth of being, yet were so simple he could use them in teaching his disciples and answering those who attacked him.

To the Pharisees he said, "I proceeded forth and came from God; neither came I of myself, but he sent me" (John 8:42). As *The New English Bible* translates it, ". . . God is the source of my being, and from him I come."

It's important to see that the Saviour's words, "I proceeded forth and came from God" do not mean that he *left* the Father. As he himself said, "He that sent me is with me: the Father hath not left me alone; for I do always those things that please him" (John 8:29).

Repeatedly when Jesus used the word "I" in such statements, he identified himself with the Christ. The Christ, manifesting to humanity the eternal truth of being, reveals man's unity with God. It brings to our apprehension the reality of man reflecting God's nature. In this understanding we find our own real selfhood. We also find healing, as Jesus proved.

Exactness of reflection

One of the fundamentals of reflection in Science is exactness. At every point and in every way the reflected image, man, coincides exactly with its source, Life, Mind, Love.

As Christ Jesus affirmed: "The Son can do nothing of himself, but what he seeth the Father do: for what things soever he doeth, these also doeth the Son likewise. For the Father loveth the Son, and sheweth him all things that himself doeth . . . . For as the Father hath life in himself; so hath he given to the Son to have life in himself" (John 5:19, 20, 26).

There is a precise correlation between this inspired explanation of source and reflection and the illustration given by Mary Baker Eddy in *Science and Health with Key to the Scriptures:* "Your mirrored reflection is your own image or likeness. If you lift a weight, your reflection does this also. If you speak, the lips of this likeness move in accord with yours. Now compare man before the mirror to his divine Principle, God. Call the mirror divine Science, and call man the reflection. Then note how true, according to Christian Science, is the reflection to its original. As the reflection of yourself appears in the mirror, so you, being spiritual, are the reflection of God" (*Science and Health*, pp. 515–516).

The reflection never deviates from its source. Any supposed deviation—into sin or sickness, darkness or deterioration, destructive action or death—is impossible in the reality of divine reflection. Whatever would present such a picture of man is illusion—totally a lie, totally unreal, a myth or self-deluded dream.

In Science man always reflects the harmony, substance, and immortality of God's nature and being. He includes and expresses all the attributes and power that belong to his perfect Father, God. He includes and expresses nothing—not a single atom or thought or condition—that deviates in the slightest from the nature of God, Spirit.

The realization of this truth is restorative because it rules out the whole catalog of sin, sickness, death. It destroys fear. It excludes suffering. It eliminates lack. None of these have any place in the infinite, perfect God; nor can they in His reflection, man. Understanding this truth, through deep and earnest prayer, restores our sense of harmonious being expressing God, our perception of our own real selfhood. The result is healing.

Completeness of reflection

Another fundamental characteristic of reflection is its completeness. In the oneness of God and His self-expression, man reflects all the action, all the intelligence, all the substance, of his Maker. The reflected image manifests every quality, element, and attribute of its original—and only these.

As reflection, the image is as complete as its original. In the words already quoted from Christ Jesus, "The Father loveth the Son, and sheweth him all things that himself doeth." All that God expresses belongs to His reflection, the true man. The infinitude of ever-outpouring Love manifesting itself, the limitless resources of Soul, the inexhaustible energies of Life, the measureless range of divine intelligence—all these are manifestations of the infinite Being; and man, as God's reflection, expresses them all.

Thus man reflects the fullness and perfection of divinity in the completeness of his own individuality, and includes no quality, no characteristic, no element that's not in the original. There's no possibility of incompleteness or deprivation in man because none exists in God. There can be no loss, want, or loneliness in man because there is none in the infinite Being he reflects.

The completeness and infinitude of Mind excludes the possibility of anything existing other than itself and its reflection. No fear can invade man's being because none exists in Mind. No destructive forces can touch man because none exist in immutable Life. God's being fills all space because He is illimitable.

Reflection is complete and infinite, manifesting the nature of the All-in-all. The effect of this truth, insofar as it holds sway in human consciousness, is to exclude any evidence of limitation, mortality, or evil. It restores, to our apprehension, the evidence of man's wholeness and perfection, seen in healing.

Consciousness and reflection

Still another fundamental of reflection is consciousness. Christ Jesus expressed this in the most profound yet the simplest of terms when he said, "As the Father knoweth me, even so know I the Father" (John 10:15).

God is conscious Being; and so we know Him as divine Mind or Ego. Because the divine Ego, God, knows His own conscious reflection, the manifestation or reflection, man, reflects this conscious knowing. In *Science and Health* Mrs. Eddy describes man as "the conscious identity of being as found in Science, in which man is the reflection of God, or Mind, and therefore is eternal . . ." (p. 475).

Thus, reflection is a thing of consciousness; indeed, the very essence of reflection *is* consciousness. In ordinary usage the word "reflection" sometimes refers to the contemplation of the contents of one's own mind or one's own mental processes. And so, in Christian metaphysics, reflection refers to the infinite Mind's contemplation of its own content. Mind knows its own reflection; and the reflection, man, is the evidence of this divine knowing.

Since this is true, man's conscious being is filled with the light of God. Did not Jesus imply this when he said, "If therefore thine eye be single, thy whole body shall be full of light" (Matt. 6:22)? This individualized spiritual consciousness is the whole of man.

We can apply this understanding in demonstrating Christian Science. In the Science of reflection, there is no unconscious, subconscious, or subliminal consciousness in man. There is only the pure light and glory, the unflawed innocence and divine purity, of Soul's eternal noonday shown forth as man's conscious being.

Since man truly reflects the divine Ego, or Mind—at every point and in every detail of his being in conformity with God's nature—there can be no evil in man's nature. When this truth is understood, it acts as spiritual law to govern our entire being. Through the Christ-power reaching humanity, this heavenly law of man's conscious goodness and perfection acts in human thought to dispel the nightmares of mortal sense and the illusion of evil. It acts as a law of recovery, a law of healing, a law of preservation, a law of progress.

We can avail ourselves of this truth in every direction. It uncovers and roots out the unseen mental cause of what may have seemed to be stubborn disease. It enables us to rid ourselves of evil traits and ugly impulses.

Because this truth of reflection is actually the universal, all-embracing law of self-expressing Principle, or Mind, we can utilize it in correcting any concept we may hold of others who seem to be ruled by anger or sensuality, selfishness or unbridled human will.

This same line of spiritual reasoning enables us to help lift the curse or mortal lie hanging over the nations, that mankind is basically both evil and good, animal as well as spiritual, and is therefore doomed to destroy itself through social disintegration or nuclear war.

In the Science of reflection, exemplified by Christ Jesus, man is the divinely illumined reflection of infinite Life and Love. His nature is good and his being immortal. He dwells within the Father, and all the Father's attributes of good dwell in him. The revelation of Christ's metaphysics, elucidated in Christian Science, is enabling us to prove in growing degree the power of this saving truth to rescue us and all humanity.

—*DeWitt John*

COUNTDOWN TO SUNRISE

I lie here quietly (long before the sky lightens
And the dawn comes) establishing who I am—
Beloved child of loving Father-Mother,
Unpressured in the equipollence of Soul,
In true being perfect as the Father in heaven is perfect.

I am cradled in eternity. No mortal history
Past, or present, or threatening in the future
Can drag me down. I am no anxious swimmer
In river where waterweeds clutch. I stand on Horeb
In clean, pure air of everlasting Truth,
Innocent in unfolding sense of Being,
Loved and loving, knowing no coming or going,
Alone, but not lonely in the infinite family of Spirit,
Secure as bird in open firmament of heaven.

I am His own, not wondering what I am;
Contented to be the expression of His I AM;
And in the marvelously clear light of this awareness,
I lightly rise to explore eternal day.

—Rosemary Cobham

Developing a Worldwide Healing Practice

*O*vercoming sickness and sin through a growing understanding of the allness of God, good, is the natural result of practicing Christian Science. But healing oneself is really just the beginning of this practice.

Progressing spiritually, a Christian Scientist not only sees the *need* for healing in larger terms, on a global scale, but he learns of his ability to expand the sphere of his own healing work and to establish a worldwide practice of Christian healing. He sees this as being in line with what Christ Jesus expected of his followers. The Master told them, "Ye are the light of the world" (Matt. 5:14). For Christian healers, Jesus' instruction and example strongly encourage an *ever-widening* reach of spiritually illumined thought.

The ability to have a far-reaching, healing impact in the world doesn't seem mysterious or unnatural when we understand that man isn't the materially-minded creature we've been educated to believe he is. His origin is Spirit, God, infinite and perfect Mind. Limited love or intelligence couldn't be characteristic of God's man, who expresses the boundless nature and power of Spirit. These limitations represent a false, mortal sense of man's abilities. Mary Baker Eddy, who discovered Christian Science, writes, "Mortals have a very imperfect sense of the spiritual man and of the infinite range of his thought" (*Science and Health with Key to the Scriptures*, p. 258). Exchanging a less-than-spiritual, less-than-perfect sense of ourselves for what's true shows us more of our unfettered ability to do good in the world.

We might be thinking, though, that we don't really have much to offer others, that our understanding of God and of His laws is too small. Perhaps we feel we barely know enough to heal everything that needs healing in our own life, let alone to be helpful to others. Yet, when Jesus instructed his students to think of themselves as light-bearers *for the world*, they were not, at that point, seasoned Christian healers and teachers themselves. Regardless of what little they may have understood of his teachings at the outset, Jesus told

them that it was light which shouldn't be hid. "Let your light so shine before men," were his words, "that they may see your good works, and glorify your Father which is in heaven" (Matt. 5:16).

Being a Christian Scientist is being spiritually-minded, having the Mind of Christ, reflecting the spirit of Christliness, the unlimited love and intelligence that come from God. Being spiritually-minded, however, is also, in a manner of speaking, being *globally*-minded. It requires dropping narrow, self-centered thinking and opening our thought to a wider affection, a universal love, and to God's omnipotence.

Divine Love impels us to do this, to love outwardly and unconditionally, not inwardly and sparingly. As we respond to Love's impulsion, we'll be more willing to respond to the needs of others. As *Christians*, we'll humbly, compassionately, fervently yearn to help our fellow beings.

Still, as we look around at the millions of people throughout the world who want help, we may feel that being able to assist them is beyond our capacity. But as Christian *Scientists*, we'll apprehend, through prayer and spiritual study, the power and allness of God, good, and the spiritual laws that underlie universal harmony. We'll recognize these laws to be present and operating everywhere, forever revealing the possibilities for achieving good.

Does developing a worldwide practice mean we need hastily to make an all-or-nothing leap from our present line of work into the full-time practice of Christian Science? No, it doesn't. Expanding the sphere of our work for humanity can develop very naturally as part of one's daily study and prayer. For example, a friend of mine, in praying to find a way to expand her practice of Christian Science, saw that she had a wonderful opportunity to do so each day through her regular study of the Bible Lesson in the *Christian Science Quarterly*. Her usual approach to the lesson had been to study each section asking herself what answers it provided for problems in her own life.

One day, however, she found herself deeply frustrated after reading a news analysis of an ongoing, violent conflict in another part of the world. It was widely believed that the atrocities in that region were inescapable because of the long history of hatred among the warring groups. At first my friend felt that with each passing day there was less and less likelihood of seeing an end to the bloodshed.

She decided to read the Bible Lesson that day to see what light its message shed on that particular situation. Her study led to the conviction that the appearance of many conflicting minds was not validated by any stubborn, long-standing belief in its reality. She saw that such a mistaken belief could be, *must* be, eradicated through an understanding of the one Mind and of man as the very expression of that Mind. It must be eradicated through the power of Christ, Truth, which is ever present and ever operative in human thought. She understood, too, that no one—*no one*—is without the God-derived ability to discern the truth of man. She knew that even in the midst of civil unrest it's possible to see past the human labels of ethnicity, social status, and so forth and feel something of the love for one's fellow beings that's natural to man as God's spiritual image.

My friend continues to read the Bible Lesson in this way, each day giving special attention to how it applies to problems in that and other areas of the world. She is finding this practice effective in offsetting many of the misconceptions underlying those problems, and in replacing them with the spiritual truths of God and man elucidated in the lesson. This also helps her cultivate a broader outlook and wider affection. She sees this Christianly scientific thinking blessing others in the many contacts she has each week, and as a rightful healing influence in the larger sphere of thought that embraces the world.

That's only one example, of course. There are many ways to expand our horizon of thought and develop a wider practice. The underlying metaphysical point is that we *are* light-bearers for the world as we strive to reflect, to some degree, the truth and love that come from God.

Spiritual progress demands that we see beyond a false, mortal sense of our abilities and accept the truth of ourselves as the unfettered expression of good; as spiritual thinkers with an ever-expanding healing practice.

—*Russ Gerber*

THE DISAPPEARANCE OF MATTER

*O*utsiders sometimes misunderstand important points of Christian metaphysics. There may be occasions when we insiders also fail to grasp adequately those same points. In fact, the more clarity and exactness Christian Scientists bring to their own perception of spiritual truths, the more they will help dissolve the mistaken views held by others. It's often easier to think in terms of straightening out the other fellow. It's a little harder when we realize that the first need is to get things perfectly straight in our own thought.

We really can't afford to take familiar truths in the Bible and Mrs. Eddy's writings for granted. The books need to be pondered—plumbed for the fullness and preciseness of their meaning. For example, what impact is made on us when we consider the fact that matter is unreal? Do we just have a vague sort of feeling that the objects around us, even the physical body itself, fall short of representing true substance? Or worse, do we perhaps move right on past such a concept, assuming that its significance belongs to the future? We can't very honestly expect humanity to perceive without study what we ourselves, even with study, still need to take hold of more fully.

Divine Science does teach unreservedly that matter must disappear in the presence of Spirit. But without explanation and application such a concept would be little more than theoretical to the Scientist and at least puzzling to the newcomer. What do we actually mean by the term "matter"? Are we thinking of the disappearance of objects around us—a bucket of paint, a piece of rope, a bag of potatoes? If so, we're floating in clouds of theory way beyond our present practice. And yet there is something very practical, very immediate, about the *present* dissolution of matter.

To the Christian metaphysician who is pondering the nature of reality, matter isn't so easily defined simply as physical items—neat little packages measured in liters, meters, and kilograms. "Matter" is actually a term that implies narrowness, confinement, limitation; it suggests a consciousness of existence that is bounded by walls of restriction. In a word, matter is mortality. And the so-called

substance that we usually think of as matter, to the extent it is subject to sudden or eventual deterioration and change, mainly *symbolizes* a state of finite thinking.

And so when we consider the unreality of matter, we're actually pondering the fact that man's true existence as the expression of immortal Spirit is limitless, boundless; our real being perpetually develops within God's infinite goodness—it isn't circumscribed by doubt or ignorance, anger or envy. We are rejecting matter when we repudiate the belief that our true life is built around such terminal concepts. We're challenging constrictive material sense itself—not merely various objects that material sense would always represent as mortal.

When we feel God's presence—experience spiritual joy, purity, integrity—we aren't losing a sense of substance; we are actually gaining a more expanded and substantial and permanent basis of existence. Real being, individual consciousness, is shaped by unrestricted qualities of God. True form, color, substance, outline, are the expression of boundless Spirit; they are not contained within the fences of mortal mentality. "Spirit and its formations are the only realities of being," our Leader, Mrs. Eddy, explains. "Matter disappears under the microscope of Spirit" (*Science and Health,* p. 264).

If one accepts matter as genuine substance, then, of course, it may seem frightening to consider relinquishing it. When one comes to realize that matter isn't some kind of reality independent of consciousness but is essentially the projection of limited thought, he will be forced to reexamine his reservations about letting go. Not that he'll automatically be glad to part with mental restrictions. People aren't easily persuaded to relinquish their imprisoning views. Mortal mind, by nature, fears the infinite because immortality, by definition, signals the demise of all belief in mortality.

But once we see that the disappearance of matter actually means the disappearance of limited thinking—of fears and impurities and willfulness—a whole new world (even a new heaven and earth) starts opening up to us. We begin more fully to understand Christ Jesus, his mission, his message, and how he was able to heal.

To some extent Jesus' very birth broke away from matter—from confining mortal concepts about man's origin. He grew to fully understand that man is not made up of limits; he is not a collection of genes bounded by the past or held within the worldly borders of illness, immorality, death. Christ Jesus recognized man's original, limitless nature as the image, even the representative, of God, divine Mind. He saw this fact with such clarity that the boundaries of illness and sin, of arrogance and death, gave way. His conviction of God's allness brought down opposing mental barriers. The Bible describes the healing effect of breaking through those false limits of matter-based thinking: a lame man walked; a child was restored to health; multitudes were fed; a sea was calmed.

Even today, as we yield to the expansiveness of Spirit, such restrictive beliefs as disease or sin, evil of every kind, break down. Matter—that is, the expression of limited and false mentality—dissolves. We experience liberation. For instance, fear gives way to the security of divine Love; spiritual vitality replaces apathy; enlightenment crowds out ignorance.

For the student of divine metaphysics, matter is daily disappearing. The flesh (cramped material-mindedness) falls before spirituality. "Limitations are put off in proportion as the fleshly nature disappears and man is found in the reflection of Spirit," writes our Leader (*Retrospection and Introspection*, p. 73). A regeneration takes place in which Christly consciousness replaces a material sense of identity. And what is the ultimate lesson offered by the Master? Was he showing us how finally to become very happy, healthy, lovable mortals? Why, of course not; he was leading us to our full salvation—out of mortality entirely.

Jesus demonstrated completely the fact that all matter, all restrictive belief, finally disappears as we fully demonstrate man's perfect expression of omniscient Mind. Man doesn't disappear. Substance doesn't disappear. Limits disappear. They come to an end because God is unbounded and man is His likeness. When Jesus ascended he gave irrefutable evidence that true being is altogether free of matter.

You and I can daily cut back the shrubbery of mortal belief that would hedge us in. Even the most modest healing is a destruction of evil; it is evidence of God's presence as described by the Psalmist, "He uttered his voice, the earth melted" (Ps. 46:6).

Even now we can give genuine meaning to the metaphysical truth that matter disappears in the light of Spirit. And finally, through spiritual regeneration and scientific healing, we will rise above all limited thought; we will reach our own ascension.

—*Nathan A. Talbot*

EVIL: "NO PORTION, NOR RIGHT, NOR MEMORIAL"

*T*he biblical story of Nehemiah rebuilding the wall of Jerusalem is a useful case history for anyone wishing to better understand the Christly way to deal with evil suggestions—with whatever would abort, hinder, divert, discourage, or defeat any good work.

When Nehemiah first heard about the broken walls and burned gates of Jerusalem, he was deeply distressed and prayed for God's guidance. As the idea for rebuilding the structure began to form, opposition to this endeavor quickly surfaced among the enemies of the Jews—Sanballat and Tobiah—for "it grieved them exceedingly that there was come a man [Nehemiah] to seek the welfare of the children of Israel" (Neh. 2:10). This is a typical response of evil—to be made distraught by the pure light of a good example and a God-directed work.

By night, and unknown to the opposition, Nehemiah carefully inspected the area. From the outset, he wisely hid his intentions and did not reveal his plans to the rulers, priests, or workers. Just so today, every righteous endeavor, every constructive work, must rest on the sure foundation of quiet reliance on God alone.

When the decision to rebuild the wall was made public, one of his opponents' early ploys was to laugh at and scorn Nehemiah's efforts. Taunting, they said: "What is this thing that ye do? will ye rebel against the king?" His response was, "The God of heaven, he will prosper us; therefore we his servants will arise and build: but ye have no portion, nor right, nor memorial, in Jerusalem" (2:19, 20).

One day, while I was reading this verse, Nehemiah's choice of the three words "portion," "right," and "memorial" seized my attention. I looked up their synonyms for an increased comprehension of their meaning. These synonyms, along with an influx of spiritual insights, revealed an expansive view of treatment in Christian Science practice.

Suddenly I could see that evil had no portion, percentage, or share in my career. Evil had no right, jurisdiction, permission, or warrant to intimidate me; nor could it hinder my spiritual progress. Evil had no memorial—no reminder or record to call itself to my attention as something that had ever dogged my steps, resulted in my history, influenced my attitudes, or caused me distress. Therefore, it could not appear as a scar (memorial) of an accident or as an emotional scar of hurt feelings. Evil could not memorialize itself in my consciousness even as a memory of someone's glance reminding me of an unpleasant incident.

Again, evil had no share of my experience to limit my strength, curb my spiritual insights, restrict my joy, deprive me of my full heritage of good from God. Evil had no warrant to threaten me with fatigue, no right to dominate my thoughts, no authority to suddenly appear as an inevitable obstacle on the pathway I was led by God to pursue.

Thus, one could declare on the basis of Nehemiah's words: There cannot remain, even in memory, a trace of evidence that evil ever had any affinity for or connection with God's spiritual man. This broad-based realization extends to one's career, body, family, church; to one's relationships with his fellow humans and with his universe.

We see in the Bible account that Nehemiah continually had to rebut evil suggestions in order to complete his project. His adversaries said of those building the wall, "They shall not know, neither see, till we come in the midst among them, and slay them, and cause the work to cease" (4:11). Here is represented the threatening attitude of evil that would victimize us or hold us hostage to its claims. Nehemiah's actions exhibit both watching and praying. This mental alertness is coupled with diligence in pursuit of the work at hand. No secret, ensnaring intention to do evil can hide from all-knowing Truth, because Truth's nature exposes the impossibility of opposite claims.

Only if one is ignorant of the deceptive nature of evil and does not understand the all-power of God can he feel thwarted or frustrated by intrusive erroneous suggestions whispered to his thought. The key to victory over evil is found in these words of Mary Baker Eddy, the Discoverer and Founder of Christian Science: "Only by admitting evil as a reality, and entering into a state of evil thoughts, can we in belief separate one man's interests from those of the whole human family, or thus attempt to separate Life from God. This is the mistake that causes much that must be repented of and overcome" (*Miscellaneous Writings*, p. 18).

A worker in her household recalled that Mrs. Eddy told her: "Whatever error you admit in yourself as real or in another, you make yourself liable to that error. Admitting error real produces error and is all there is to it" (*We Knew Mary Baker Eddy* [Boston: The Christian Science Publishing Society, 1979], p. 202).

So we are taught never to admit the reality of evil. We neither personify nor personalize evil, for we are not engaged in a mental game of "Pin the [Tale]" on someone! This consistent, upright position would effectually annihilate gossip, vilification, slander, meddlesomeness, and destructive criticism.

The insistent nature of evil is also represented in the Bible story. Sanballat and Geshem sought to do more mischief by requesting a meeting with Nehemiah in an outlying village. Nehemiah's wisdom enabled him to see this as an effort to disrupt the progress of the work. He refused such requests on four occasions—each time with an insightful rejection of the entreaty and a rededication to the God-directed endeavor. Four times they tried and four times he remained steadfast and faithful to his divine purpose, refusing to be sidetracked.

Nehemiah's swift, persistent rebuttals (based on prayer to God and on spiritual understanding) made him superior to every subterfuge and threat of evil that would have halted the work. He resisted at every point and was strengthened. Like Nehemiah, we too can unswervingly respond by affirming good and unhesitatingly rejecting every evil intimation, whether it comes as gossip, rumor, innuendo, false witness, or other intrigue.

The fifth time, an open letter was sent to Nehemiah by his enemies in an attempt to misrepresent or pervert his genuine purpose in rebuilding the wall and thereby cause him to be afraid. Their defamatory statements hinted that Nehemiah was working for self-glorification, that he was a rebel who wished to be king. To provide a smoke screen for its activities, evil charges others with its own base motives, thus seeking to draw attention elsewhere. These twisted statements were met with Nehemiah's prayer, "Now therefore, O God, strengthen my hands" (Neh. 6:9). Today, evil's repeated challenges require ever stronger commitment from workers dedicated to spiritual living.

The wall was successfully rebuilt. Nehemiah had shown that the work of God was not to be checked or thwarted, and that His faithful servants could not be intimidated.

In summary, we can see many methods of error exhibited in this story: ridicule, scorn, hatred, persistent intimidation, falsehood, rumor, slander, relentless desire to defeat the purpose of good. As we follow Nehemiah's example, we are assured that spiritual-mindedness prevents deception by any of error's subtle methods. The result of such alertness is the strengthening of God's servant and the certain defeat of evil.

We are effectual workers as we manifest Nehemiah-like qualities, always letting God direct our careers. Only then can we safely advance and flourish. Mrs. Eddy, author of the Christian Science textbook, *Science and Health with Key to the Scriptures,* writes: "Eternal harmony, perpetuity, and perfection, constitute the phenomena of being, governed by the immutable and eternal laws of God; whereas matter and human will, intellect, desire, and fear, are not the creators, controllers, nor destroyers of life or its harmonies" (*No and Yes,* pp. 10–11).

—*Carolyn E. Holte*

GIDEON'S THREE HUNDRED

The time once came when the children of Israel had urgent need to learn a lesson. Left without a leader after the passing away of Joshua, they so lapsed into evil ways that they at last found themselves fugitives in the land of Midian, hiding in dens and caves in the mountains for fear of the depredations of those around them. This they endured for seven miserable years; then, as had so often happened, in their dire extremity they "called upon the Lord," and He sent them a deliverer.

When Gideon, at the divine command, left his father's threshing field to become their leader, he was confronted with a somewhat unique situation, for he found that the thirty-two thousand unhappy, frightened fugitives so far exceeded the Midianites in number that they might easily at any time, but for their fears, have asserted their freedom. Even under their new leader, however, they were not to depend upon numerical supremacy for their ultimate release. The mere incident of numbers weighed not one whit in the balances of God; and that was the lesson which they had need to learn, lest in their newfound courage following Gideon's appearance they should "vaunt themselves," and say, "Mine own hand hath saved me" (Judges 7:2). And the way in which they were taught this lesson was indeed a strange one.

The decisive hour had arrived. On one side of the hill were the Midianites, and not far from them the camp of Israel, "beside the well of Harod;" (Judges 7:1) but before the fighting was allowed to begin, those of the Israelites who were afraid were told to depart. Whereupon "there returned of the people twenty and two thousand" (v. 3). The ten thousand remaining were then told to go to the water's edge and drink. "And the Lord said unto Gideon, Every one that lappeth of the water with his tongue, as a dog lappeth, him shalt thou set by himself; likewise every one that boweth down upon his knees to drink. And the number of them that lapped, putting their hand to their mouth, were three hundred men: but all the rest of the people bowed down upon their knees to drink water. And the Lord said unto Gideon, By the three hundred men that lapped will I save you."

Viewed superficially, this whole proceeding seems strangely inconsequential at so critical a moment, but to the thoughtful Bible student it contains a deep and beautiful significance. It is readily seen that the real intent was to test each man's fidelity, to discover how much interest he took in the work before him; to find out, in other words, not in what manner he would drink, but whether he cared to drink at all, with the enemy in plain sight and the battle imminent. Therefore we find that those who were chosen were those who would not stop long enough to kneel down beside the well and drink quietly and comfortably, but who, in their eagerness to hasten the attack, quickly dashed up the water with their hands and hurried on. No wonder the host of Midian fled! Gideon's "three hundred" stands for that high quality of mental alertness which always wins. Not by the twenty-two thousand who were afraid, nor by the ten thousand who were indifferent, but by the three hundred who rushed on to meet the foe, were the Israelites delivered.

There is a subtle mesmerism in numbers to which the Christian Scientist has constant need to keep himself awake. Our wise Leader has even considered the matter of sufficient importance to make it the subject of a by-law, wherein she directs the members of The Mother Church to "turn away from personality and numbering the people" (*Church Manual*, Art. VIII, Sect. 28). One cannot afford to be lured into the belief that in numbers there is strength, nor into the opposite and equally erroneous belief that in lack of numbers there is weakness. One right thought has more activity, power, and impulsion than any number of wrong thoughts, no matter how often or how vehemently expressed. If every one in the world were to shout at the same moment, "The world is flat," it would not make it flat. One single voice replying, "The world is round," would have more power, because it has more truth than a whole world's mistaken impotence.

The remembrance of this should surely inspire all of us with fresh courage, but especially those students of Christian Science who happen to be living in small places, where the workers comprise but a handful, and who sometimes perhaps give way to a sense of discouragement as they climb the narrow stairs, week after week, to the little room where their services are held. They think the cause of Christian Science is weak in that town because the Scientists themselves are so few. "What can you do," the adversary whispers, "among so many?" The disciples once succumbed to the same suggestion (John 6:9). They brought to Jesus the five loaves and the two small fishes, and then, looking at the multitude waiting to be fed, one of them asked helplessly, "But what are they among so many?" Yet the multitude were fed, because the Master looked beyond the limitation of numbers into the realm of infinite possibilities.

The multitude today, those starving for the bread of Life, may be fed in like manner, if those faithful followers of the Christ in that little room up the narrow stairs will forget the loaves and the fishes to contemplate instead Love's ever-present abundance. In the throng of long ago that had followed the Master out into the desert place, there must have been quite as much ignorance, intolerance, superstition, prejudice, antagonism, and opposition as seems to exist in the average small town of the present time, yet Jesus fed them all. If he had stopped to pity himself because he was "one," and they were "five thousand," would there have been twelve baskets of fragments remaining over and above all that had been eaten?

Some one has defined the need of the moment as "not more Christian Scientists, but better ones." Then let us look up and rejoice. That little room where "two or three are gathered together," may be the very chrysalis from which some radiant butterfly will one day rise to find its wings. Have not wonderful things grown from just such modest beginnings? Do we not all know of "an upper room" where a little company once gathered to sup and talk together, as friends will on the eve of a separation? It could not have been much to look at, from a material point of view, and those who met there were but twelve in number; yet there went forth from that memorable meeting, a message which has revolutionized the world.

With the worker in the large city, however, the mesmerism of numbers takes a radically different form. He has his beautiful church, his well-appointed reading-room, his convenient practitioner, and the respect if not the unqualified approval of the community in general. He is no longer the subject of persecution and ridicule, nor considered to be of unsound mind because he refuses to call a doctor when he is sick. In fact, everything seems to be going along so nicely that if he is not careful he is sometimes lulled into a pleasant state of self-satisfied apathy. In the small town the adversary whispers, "There are so few, how can you do anything?" In the large town he says,

"There are so many, why need you do anything?" But it is the same adversary, and we need to recognize it in whatever outward garb it comes to us, for its purpose is ever to beguile us into the inaction which would tend to check the steady progress of our cause.

There is no simpler way to put a man to sleep, figuratively speaking, than to make him think that there is no particular reason for him to keep awake. Even the disciples once listened to this suggestion. It was in the garden of Gethsemane, and although Jesus had asked them to watch with him "one hour" (Matt. 26:40), as soon as he had left them they were straightway overcome with slumber. Is it not possible that each man allowed himself to fall asleep partly because he was so sure that all the rest would keep awake? Yet it ended in all quietly sleeping at the very time that their help was most needed; for just a step away, in the purple shadows of the moonlit olive trees, their beloved Master was kneeling, in lonely agony, "his sweat . . . as it were great drops of blood falling down to the ground" (Luke 22:44).

Let us not be deceived by numbers. When the cause of Christian Science becomes in any locality what may be termed, for want of a better word, "popular," and great crowds flock to its doors, it is not wise for the Christian Scientist to relax his vigilance. Popularity is often a crucial testing-time for churches as well as for individuals, and in our natural desire to see our church grow, let us not lose sight of the fact that much untried material hastily and over-zealously added to our church-membership does not always facilitate the orderly and dignified progress of the church body as a whole. The wise captain does not overload his ship.

The ship was overloaded once in the third century of the Christian era, when Constantine thought to increase the brilliancy of his reign by adding Christianity, like another jewel, to the imperial crown. The gay world of Rome accepted it, not because they loved it, but because an emperor had made it popular. We all know the result. Church and state became hopelessly intermingled, politics and personality crept in, and a little later the purity and simplicity of the Christ-message was lost, smothered in the superheated atmosphere of unthinking numbers. Its true animus, the healing power which ever characterized the earlier workers, was forgotten, until, centuries later, one woman lived close enough to God to find this "pearl of great price" and to restore its primitive luster. Did the mesmerism of numbers disturb our Leader, Mrs. Eddy? She never faltered, although the little town of Lynn, Massachusetts, once held the only student of Christian Science in all the world.

Should we not rejoice to remember these things, we in our handsome finished churches, and we in our little rooms up the narrow stairs? Gideon's "three hundred" is here today, for it simply means a condition of thought expressed in fidelity, in love, in earnestness, in consecration, in steadfast devotion. It is quality rather than quantity. It is that for which Mrs. Eddy once sent out an imperative call, sweetly insistent as some silver trumpet-tone whose echoes still linger in hearts attuned to hear. These were her words as found in *Miscellaneous Writings* (p. 176): "Are we duly aware of our own great opportunities and responsibilities? . . . Never was there a more solemn and imperious call than God makes to us all, right here, for fervent devotion and an absolute consecration to the greatest and holiest of all causes. The hour is come. The great battle of Armageddon is upon us. ... What will you do about it? ... Will you doff your lavender-kid zeal, and become real and consecrated warriors? Will you give yourselves wholly and irrevocably to the great work of establishing the truth, the gospel, and the Science which are necessary to the salvation of the world from error, sin, disease, and death? Answer at once and practically, and answer aright!" And Gideon's "three hundred" answered.

—*Louise Knight Wheatley*

THE GLORY "BEFORE THE WORLD WAS"

"And now, O Father, glorify thou me with thine own self with the glory which I had with thee before the world was" (John 17:5). These words were not uttered by a triumphant potentate returning from conquest, but by a man about to experience crucifixion for his goodness. They were not spoken in a time when peace reigned throughout the civilized world, but when cruelty, injustice, persecution, aggression, and wickedness stalked the earth. This remarkable statement was made in a country where racial hatreds permeated religious doctrines, political actions, and governmental decrees. They were made by one "despised and rejected of men," (Isaiah 53:3) yet they have lived in the hearts of men through all the ages that followed. They were spoken in the shadow of a cross, but fulfilled in the resurrection of Jesus Christ.

Shortly before Jews and Romans, politicians and soldiers, priests and populace, united to attempt the destruction of the temporal life of this just man, he had declared that he had power to give eternal life to as many as God had given him. When carnality was boasting that it would end his mission, destroy his existence, and rob him of all holy fame, he knew that he was being glorified by the power that was primeval, eternal, universal Love. He asked not for glory from the world, but for the glory "before the world was" (John 17:5). Could physical force prevent the answer to this request? Could human hatred shut him out from the presence of his Father? Could the world intervene between eternal Life and its infolded manifestation?

Jesus' utterance of this remarkable prayer indicates that he knew that right then and there Life was keeping man at the point of perfection. He was declaring that divinity at that moment was causing the facts of eternal Life to appear in man, who is always the spiritual son of God, and was bringing this truth to human consciousness. He was virtually repeating his declaration, "And no man hath ascended up to heaven, but he that came down from heaven, even the Son of man which is in heaven" (John 3:13). No power could keep the man who was in heaven out of heaven.

The glory "before the world was" meant to Jesus the ability of eternal Life forever to preserve in man the bliss of Spirit's paradise, "a spiritual sense of Life and power," as Mrs. Eddy writes in *Miscellaneous Writings* (p. 70). It proclaimed the action of divine law, holding man inseparable from God, not abandoning him to annihilation. This glory was existence in and of Spirit, where the capacities and opportunities of the infinite are forever expressed in man. This meant eternal unfolding as the conscious identity of indestructible Being.

Our Leader states that "infinite progression is concrete being, which finite mortals see and comprehend only as abstract glory. As mortal mind, or the material sense of life, is put off, the spiritual sense and Science of being is brought to light" (*Miscellaneous Writings*, p. 82). At the moment when the carnal mind was believing that the career of the man Jesus was ending, he was aware of and claiming "infinite progression" as the glory constantly given to man by his divine Father. He claimed this not as something new to which he would later attain, but as the state in which man eternally abides with God; as that which the world had never disturbed or altered.

Our Master's radiancy of conscious at-one-ment with God, finding expression in the holy words of John 17:5, shone out of the deepest time of gloom the earth might ever know. The Christ, Truth, was about to be repudiated by secular and religious rulers; the man who had taught and demonstrated the divine power was to be crucified, and his disciples scattered. Friends were going to betray, enemies slander, and the would-be forces of suppositional evil seem to unite to blot out the name and teaching of Jesus Christ from the earth. The insidious methods of enthroned wickedness were to attempt to banish Christianity from the hearts and thoughts of men. The power of God was to be openly scorned and ridiculed by the masses, possibly including some whom Jesus had healed. Yet, our Way-shower, knowing that all this would come to pass, standing on the very threshold of its threatened cataclysm, said, "And now, O Father, glorify thou me with thine own self with the glory which I had with thee before the world was."

In this utterance Jesus virtually declared that he was ready to let the spiritual man appear where the mortal had seemed to be; to let the Son of God replace the son of Mary; to let the selfhood of the infinite and eternal dispel the appearance of the finite and temporal. He was aware that the human was ready to yield to the divine at every point. He was ready to relinquish all the beliefs of life, substance, and intelligence in matter, and so necessarily experience the appearing of spiritual man in the likeness of God. He knew that error was only working out its own uncovering and destruction, while he was dwelling with the Science of divine Principle and its perpetual peace.

By patient, persistent steps of understanding and overcoming, the gentle, mighty Nazarene had trod the path from sense to Soul for more than thirty years. He knew the last and greatest assault of seeming evil could not overthrow the spiritual gain of previous achievements, but that this accumulated evidence of divine power with him would silence forever, in his pure consciousness, the last whisper of a power opposed to God. The facts of spiritual existence were more real to him than the shadows of materiality. The glory of divine selfhood was more vivid to his thought than the gloom of mortal sense. He trusted divinity to encompass humanity in its unquestionable demonstration of omnipotence.

This trust was not misplaced. Jesus' prayer was answered and his work finished. The cries of "Crucify him" were swallowed up in the undying sweetness of the Master's words: "Peace I leave with you, my peace I give unto you: not as the world giveth, give I unto you. Let not your heart be troubled, neither let it be afraid" (John 14:27). Entombment was followed by resurrection, and the succeeding forty days by ascension. The vitality of his teachings and demonstrations has increased through all the centuries and come into fulfillment of prophecy in Christian Science, which is teaching every man to wake to the glory of his true identity as the son of God.

Christian Science, the Science which Jesus taught and lived, declares that "the primal facts of being are eternal; they are never extinguished in a night of discord" (*Miscellaneous Writings*, p. 187). This clear echo of the teaching of the Way-shower comes to heavy hearts today, pointing the path to harmony. No matter how deep the darkness of mortal experience may seem to be, no matter how aggressive the arguments of error may have become, no matter how cruel are the circumstances which seem to engulf, it is the time for the faithful one to pray, "And now, O Father, glorify thou me with thine own self with the glory which I had with thee before the world was." The primal fact of man's oneness with God has not been destroyed by error's seeming. The power of omnipotent and omnipresent good is unchanged, and is able to lift

our stumbling into soaring. Today, as in Jesus' time, divine Love can bring to human comprehension the Life that is God, and the man who is the beloved of God, even the true, eternal selfhood of everyone.

The same truth which lifted Jesus above the sense of impending doom, and conquered it, says to the saddened or discouraged heart today:

Mourner, it calls you,—'Come to my bosom,
Love wipes your tears all away,
And will lift the shade of gloom,
And for you make radiant room
Midst the glories of one endless day.'

(*Poems* by Mary Baker Eddy, p. 75.)

Divine Love does not keep men struggling through days of deprivation and despair, but lifts them into Spirit's "endless day," where there is "radiant room" for all. But we note that the admonition to come to the bosom of Love precedes the statement of Love's tender ministration. This means the recognition of God's presence with man, the recognition of man's spiritual selfhood as the son of God, the yielding of the human, material sense of things to divine Truth. This human approach to eternal reality should not be difficult or apprehensive, for the word "bosom" indicates that reality is Mother-Love, ready at the slightest touch to respond with comfort and satisfaction, to impart the very essence of divine harmony immediately to the needy one.

There is no "shade of gloom" so dense that it cannot be dispelled by the glory of spiritual Truth. There is no seeming danger so imminent that it cannot be proved powerless through the understanding of divine Love. There is no threat of evil that cannot be silenced by the Word of God. There are not two powers, good and evil, but only one—good. In this infinite good man lives, moves, and has eternal existence. Because Jesus knew this truth, it revealed itself in his case in ever-increasing degree until it became the all-in-all of his being. The same privilege belongs to everyone today who will study and apply the teachings of Jesus as unfolded in Christian Science.

The darkest hour in human experience presents the opportunity to turn away from materiality to divine reality, from the finite to the infinite. It is the moment in which human consciousness may close the door of mortal sense, and open wide to spiritual understanding. At this point the claim of association with evil may be dismissed, and the indissoluble relationship between God and man realized. Thought can become aware of what God is able to do for His beloved, rather than of what error threatens to be able to do to the supposed object of its hate. At such a time the world of sense gives place to the heaven of Soul.

The darkest hour divinely illumined is when our fields are white for harvest to be garnered into the "radiant room" of spiritual realization, not to be destroyed by the false reaper, death. This, and more, is what Jesus implied in his statement of man's God-given glory. This is what Christian Science is demonstrating to faithful hearts in this age, reiterating and repeating the Christ-salvation. The hearts of men need not be troubled or afraid. The glory "before the world was," is, and will still be when the mortal sense of the world has passed away.

—*Julia M. Johnston*

GOD'S PROVISION AND LAUNCHING OUT "INTO THE DEEP"

Simon, James, and John were business partners. Luke's Gospel tells us of an occasion when they had worked hard—all night, in fact—but human skill, talent, experience, and a strong work ethic had not been productive. Looking at this account in today's business terms, one might say that the fish were their product, the boats were the capital, the sea was the location, Simon was the management, the others were the staff. Theoretically, each of the elements for business success was in place, but the future disciples' business was failing. They had caught no fish. They had done the best they knew how to do, but there were no returns. Perhaps they were fighting depression, stress, and fatigue. What was needed? Retraining? A new product? Modernization? Layoffs? Shutdowns?

Christ Jesus, understanding the divine source and nature of true substance, came onto the scene, discerned the soon-to-be disciples' thought, and directed their action. The Bible tells us: "He said unto Simon, Launch out into the deep, and let down your nets for a draught. And Simon answering said unto him, Master, we have toiled all the night, and have taken nothing: nevertheless at thy word I will let down the net. And when they had this done, they enclosed a great multitude of fishes: and their net brake. And they beckoned unto their partners, which were in the other ship, that they should come and help them. And they came, and filled both the ships, so that they began to sink" (Luke 5:4–7).

It is interesting to note that even though the basic elements of the business remained the same—the management, the product, the staff, and the location—the business was a success when the enlightening, saving influence of Christ, Truth, which Jesus embodied, was brought to bear on the situation and effected a change of thought. The difference was seen when the businessmen were willing to put discouragement and human reasoning aside and follow Jesus' instruction to "launch out into the deep"—or in other words, to launch *thought* out. Out—away from commonly held, fragile, or shallow human reasoning into the pure depths of spiritual thinking. *Science and Health* by

Mary Baker Eddy states, "We must look deep into realism instead of accepting only the outward sense of things" (*Science and Health*, p. 129). It is deep, spiritual thinking that is most needed to meet successfully the aggressive threats of financial restriction that would keep us from pursuing worthy aspirations and goals.

When we are looking deep into realism, it is helpful to take a moment and ask ourselves, "Where am I believing my supply comes from?" Does it come from my monthly paycheck? Does it come from a husband or husband's job, a wife or wife's job? Is it determined by the success of my company? Does supply come from pensions, mutual funds, stocks, certificates of deposit, or high-interest-bearing securities? Is supply from an inheritance? Is it determined by how many clients or patients I have?

As much as it may look as though these things are the actual sources of our provision, they are not. They may be useful and appropriate means for seeing evidence of God's provision, but they are not the source itself. In the final analysis, supply does not come from the shallow waters of materialism. It doesn't come from strategies or even from human frugality. When we launch out deep into the perception of spiritual reality, we discover that all good, all substance, is from God, who is infinite Mind. God is conscious of His own infinitude. Man, as the spiritual reflection of God, is conscious only of infinite, unrestricted being, and is inseparable from God's provision. Neither infinite Mind nor its expression, man, knows limitation, stress, or encumbered being. And because man is spiritual, his supply is spiritually based.

Just as the sun shines, so infinite provision is continuously imparted from God to man. Supply is actually God's thoughts and ideas. These cannot be blocked, restricted, or depressed in any way. Unlike the variableness of the human economy, the flowing of Spirit's ideas is invariable, without cycles or delay.

To discern and demonstrate these truths requires letting go of old habits of thinking, even thinking patterned after others in our family, company, or community. It requires a new alertness to suggestions of limitation and a willingness to actively and consistently dismiss these thoughts as illegitimate, since they are not from God. It requires that we yield, wholeheartedly, sometimes in the face of extreme circumstances, to the fundamental truth that all is infinite, unrestricted Mind and its unlimited expression. This mental "[launching] … into the deep" heals a multitude of financial fears and pressures. It also heals the tendency to ruminate over past situations where severe lack seemed to have existed. The spiritual fact is that a condition of limitation or poverty was never known to God. Times of apparent inadequacy were nothing more than the manifestation of mesmerized human thought.

It is the Christ that gives us the ability to see through this mesmerism. The saving Christ, revealing the truth of God to human consciousness, awakens us to the opportunities immediately available. The Christ dispels intense fears and destroys the solid convictions of traditional thinking that would rationalize and confirm lack.

In her *Miscellaneous Writings*, Mrs. Eddy states, "God gives you His spiritual ideas, and in turn, they give you daily supplies" (p. 307). God's ideas are constantly pouring forth, bringing inspiration, comfort, strength, insight. His ideas lead us to ways of blessing others, of expressing greater creativity and productivity. It is animal magnetism, the supposed pull of materialistic thinking, that would have us believe we are incapable of perceiving God's ideas. Through prayer we can know with conviction that not only does God impart His ideas and liberating thoughts, but He also provides us with the energy and wisdom and love in our hearts to *act* upon these ideas and intuitions. He gives us the motivation, desire, and strength to follow through with them.

Understanding God's ever-available abundance in our lives does not mean, however, that we should be wasteful. It is not a license for extravagance or for fiscal or environmental irresponsibility. Nor does it allow for arrogance or exclusivity. These elements of mortal thought are ultimately destructive. Rather, launching out into the deep requires the cultivation of humility and the ability to manage our resources wisely, especially our *mental* resources. So, it is of vital importance that we understand the difference between an expense and an investment.

If we have an expense, we give out money and expect never to see it again. We get no funds back. When we have an investment, we expect to get a return on our funds. An expensive thought is one that provides no return. A thought that is a good investment gets a good return.

So, what are expensive thoughts? Ruminating about the past, worrying about the future, thoughts of envy, resentment, gossip, guilt—these are expensive because they separate us from perceiving God's spiritual ideas. They bring no good return. Forgiving thoughts, pure thoughts, expectant thoughts, Christly thoughts—these are thoughts that bring a good return.

We must check our thinking. We might be surprised to discover just how expensive our thinking is! What is it that we can't afford? We can't afford to seek out sensual or violent thoughts for entertainment. This thinking is too expensive. Self-justification, willfulness, condemnation, pride, and selfishness are too expensive. We can't even afford to be afraid—or in other words, to expect evil. Fear is nonproductive. It is far too expensive. Are we using our mental resources for expense or for investment?

The Bible states that we should think upon the things that are true, honest, just, pure, lovely, and of good report (see Phil. 4:8). Why? Because they are good investments.

An investment that always brings a good return is spiritualization, or purification, of thought. In this regard, people sometimes deprive themselves of the Christian Science treatment, the spiritual means that will heal them. Through such treatment, thought is purified to some degree and lives are blessed. Of course, it's always appropriate and progressive for people to apply God's laws and pray for themselves. Sometimes, however, people don't get spiritual help from another when they need assistance in spiritualizing their thought, because they believe they can't afford it. Financial limitations should never keep one from getting the help he or she needs from either a Christian Science nurse or a practitioner. We can afford spiritual growth. It does not drain but only enriches. Think about what we can't afford. We can't afford apathy, stagnation, procrastination with error, or continued mesmerism.

A businessman I know discovered the healing returns from properly investing his thoughts. He owned a company that was struggling financially and was not getting enough business. After calling a practitioner for Christian Science treatment, he said that he "once and for all fully 'squared off' against the lie about lack of money." He continued: "I mentally and even aloud talked with God, telling Him that I knew He always hears my prayers. I said I knew *absolutely* that He is all there is, and that His plan for me did not include any form of lack or insufficiency."

The man then began to make good investments with his mental resources. He explained: "I expressed gratitude for all of the many evidences of God's goodness that I have experienced in my life, including my wife, my son, my career, and the many healings I've had. I really focused on gratitude. The more I did this, the more I saw that the freedom from financial insufficiency I was seeking had already been achieved. Worry about the future began fading away, and I became calm and expectant of good."

Within a short time he began receiving calls from old customers and potential new customers. His company has continued to be prosperous. He launched his thought out into the deep, so to speak, gained a better sense of what supply really is, and invested his thoughts wisely. He cut way back on expensive thinking, and he gave his consent to the fact that God is the abundant provider of all good.

When Simon launched out into the deep, he didn't catch a meager amount—there was superabundance. His nets were overflowing. Jesus had addressed this fisherman's fear and changed the entire direction of his life. When he was willing to forsake all—all materialistic goals and thinking—and put his trust in Spirit, he saw proof of God's constant provision.

We need never live within the boundaries set by the mortal, carnal mind—including financial boundaries. Boundaries are all mortal mind knows. We don't have to believe them! When we launch out into the deep and claim the infinite Mind as our Mind because we are God's own reflection, we'll realize that all the provision we need is forever ours.

—*Jan Kassahn Keeler*

THE GOSPEL OF LOVE—*LIVED*

❦

*D*ivine Love heals because it is pure good. Love has no evil element. This Love, God, is not only untouched by evil; by reason of its allness, Love rules evil out—gives it no way or place to exist or operate. The divine Principle, Love, is the only creator, and all that Love creates is good, reflecting Love. The purpose of man—God's spiritual image and likeness—is to reflect Love, in all its purity and goodness.

One reason people like to pray, and to ponder the Word of God, is that they are so hungry for this good news. That's what the word *gospel* means—good message, good story, good news. The life and ministry of Christ Jesus, which the Bible tells us about in its four Gospels, deliver the reassuring message of God's pure goodness, and of His unwavering love for each one of us, His children. To give oneself time, through prayer and Bible study, to take this good message into one's consciousness and assimilate it is like inhaling a purifying, life-giving breath of mental fresh air. But to feel the full impact of this gospel, or good news, of Love, and to be a healing influence in the world, we need to do more than take a few breaths of Love into our consciousness. We let Love *fill* our hearts and minds with a spiritual understanding of and love for God and His creation. We let it remove from our mental homes all that is impure, ungodlike. We let God, and not the world, shape our thoughts, desires, and characters from moment to moment.

Jesus did this. It was through his purity—his faithful reflection of divine Love in every thought and act—that the gospel of Love reached others, that it inspired and healed them. And Jesus expected his followers to bring the gospel message to others, so that they might experience inspiration and healing. He said, "Go ye into all the world, and preach the gospel to every creature" (Mark 16:15). But how?

Words of themselves, whether heard or read, don't heal. Healing occurs when human consciousness is transformed by Christ, Truth. Healing occurs when God's love for us is concretely felt—when the *spirit* of divine Love is communicated. If we want to share the good news of God's love, the most fundamental thing we can do is to *live* it. Then the gospel of Love, which communicates and heals, will be felt.

Mary Baker Eddy knew the value of following Jesus' example of letting God's love fill one's consciousness and shape one's life. Her healing ability didn't come just from her *discovery* of the Science of Christ; it came from her *living* of the gospel of Love. And everything she wrote on Christian practice points others in this direction. In the book of By-Laws she wrote to guide the members of her Church—the *Manual of The Mother Church*—she gave this instruction to those who read from the Bible and *Science and Health with Key to the Scriptures* in the worship services of branch churches and of The Mother Church: "They must keep themselves unspotted from the world,—uncontaminated with evil,—that the mental atmosphere they exhale shall promote health and holiness, even that spiritual *animus* so universally needed" (*Manual*, Art. III, Sect. 1).

It does take devotion of thought to keep one's consciousness filled with Love, and to let Love alone govern us. The world can mightily test one's faithfulness. It certainly tested Mrs. Eddy. But she remained "unspotted from the world,—uncontaminated with evil." The mental atmosphere she exhaled did "promote health and holiness." Being a prominent figure—having challenged the traditional thinking of the ages in regard to science, theology, and medicine—she was often the target of unjust attacks from many quarters. At one time, when she was faced with a lawsuit that challenged her very integrity, and reporters were continually pressing to see her, a particularly hostile group of newsmen came specifically to dig up something sensational.

Mrs. Eddy had given her secretary, Irving C. Tomlinson, the job of taking calls from the press. He wrote, in a book about his years of service to Mrs. Eddy: "The chief man among this group, representing a big New York newspaper, was known as a particularly hard-boiled reporter and a steady drinker. He had been afflicted for some years with a cancerous growth of the throat, which was extremely painful and at times overwhelmed him completely.

"One evening as they were all sitting in his room at the Eagle Hotel, drinking and smoking, bored with their stay, this man was suffering with his throat; he had lost his voice entirely and was unable to speak a word. Mrs. Eddy had asked me to call these men by telephone and inform them that it was impossible for her to see them. But she cautioned me at the same time, 'Be sure to ask for the leading man and speak directly to him.'"

When Mr. Tomlinson called, he was told that the head man could not come to the phone because he could not speak. Mrs. Eddy—who characteristically embraced even her enemies in the impartial, universal love of God—had told Mr. Tomlinson to insist that he come; he could at least listen to the message Tomlinson was to deliver to him from her. He came grudgingly, and listened. He was healed. Tomlinson continues: "The healing stirred these men. … [They] had believed Mrs. Eddy to be only a humbug, and the reputed healings of Christian Science to be a great hoax. Their whole position was overthrown by this proof offered before their very eyes. They packed their bags and left.

"Some years later a relative of this man called at my office in Boston, and gave me the following message: 'My uncle requested me to see you and to tell you that in his last days he turned to Christian Science, and he knew that he owed a debt of gratitude to Mrs. Eddy for his healing in Concord.'" (*Twelve Years with Mary Baker Eddy* [Boston: The Christian Science Board of Directors, 1966], pp. 63–65.) Such is the power of divine Love lived.

Whatever we inhale, we exhale. In proportion as divine Love and its purifying activity is welcomed into our consciousness and life, it is felt in the mental atmosphere we exhale. The spirit of Love is felt in inspiration and healing. The gospel of Love is preached through our *living* of it.

—*Barbara M. Vining*

GRACE, HEALING, AND GOD'S UNFAILING LOVE

◇

*H*ave you ever felt there might be something more you needed to do to deserve God's love? Or that the way you've lived in the past has earned you a place *outside* of God's love? To these questions, divine grace brings an answer of comfort and peace.

As I've considered the whole subject of grace, I've come to feel that God simply loves us all—no matter what. From the standpoint of Christian Science, if God *is* Love, if He is infinite, eternal, omnipresent divine Love, then all that God can possibly do is to *be* that Love. He can only love us with an infinite, boundless capacity, throughout all time, and everywhere. This love exists for each of us quite independently of anything we might ever do in this present sphere of existence.

We really can't *win* God's love, and we certainly can't *lose* God's love—any more than our actions could win or lose the sunshine on a cloudless summer day. The same sunshine is present for everyone, without limit or personal restriction, because the nature of the sun is always to shine, universally and impartially—and not just at noonday when no clouds are present. And likewise, we live every moment in the light of God's love. We take sustenance from it. We gain the meaning and purpose of our lives from it. God's love, experienced through His grace, is, in fact, the very reason for our existence and the greatest thing our lives were ever intended for. We live *for* Love, and we live *to* love.

Does this concept seem impractical or without direct application to the success of our lives? Consider this: what if a businessman … or a schoolteacher … or a factory worker … or a homemaker … or the president of the most powerful nation on earth saw his or her own life's meaning and purpose to be *the expression of divine Love?* Would that have a direct impact on human affairs? Would it change anything? Rather, what would *not* be impacted? What would *not* be changed? To me, this is the promise of divine grace—that everything is changed, transformed, by Love and its expression.

God's grace has been basic to Christian theology since the earliest days of Jesus and his disciples. In the Bible, the Apostle Paul often writes on the subject. Paul's epistles regularly open and close with salutations and benedictions of grace. For example, in the tradition of Paul, the New Testament letter to the Hebrews declares, "For it is a good thing that the heart be established with grace" (Heb. 13:9).

From firsthand experience Paul knew much about the grace of God. Hadn't he felt divine Love's chastening touch as he made his way toward Damascus? Grace saved Paul that day—and who, we might ask, ever deserved it less than this persecutor of Jesus' followers? The effect of grace was literally to change him from Saul to Paul, lifting him from one who judged and condemned Christians to a God-appointed teacher, preacher, and healer. Paul now followed in the footsteps of the Master, Christ Jesus. And he knew his newly found mission was a direct result of the transforming grace of God. "For I am the least of the apostles," he would later write, "that am not meet to be called an apostle, because I persecuted the church of God. But by the grace of God I am what I am" (I Cor. 15:9, 10).

Paul's words offer a powerful promise for each of us—that no matter what wrongs we may have done or thought, grace can transform us even now—even on our own road to Damascus. And then God's grace gives us what we need to live with purer motives and affection—to accomplish all the good we are capable of.

The Greek word in the New Testament writings for grace is *charis*. One Bible authority notes that the root meaning includes "*the gladdening, joy-bringing,*" and that the Greeks commonly saluted one another with "Joy to you!" (The Christians would come to greet one another with "Grace to you!") The same reference continues: "There is little in earlier phraseology [before the Christian era] to explain the supremacy in the NT [New Testament] of this specific term; a new experience demanded a new name. 'Grace' designates *the principle in God of man's salvation through Jesus Christ. It is God's unmerited, unconstrained love towards sinners, revealed and operative in Christ.*" (See James Hastings, *Dictionary of the Bible* [New York: Charles Scribner's Sons, 1948], p. 313.) Another Bible reference expands the definition of *charis* (grace) as "the divine influence upon the heart, and its reflection in the life." (James Strong, "Greek Dictionary of the New Testament," *Strong's Exhaustive Concordance of the Bible*, p. 77.)

As we welcome this divine influence into our lives, we'll come to see that our whole life can actually be a prayer of grace. Prayer isn't just those times that we set aside with hands clasped. We really do pray with our lives. So, a central question we might ask ourselves is, "What kind of prayer am I living?" The Discoverer of Christian Science, Mary Baker Eddy, observed: "To live so as to keep human consciousness in constant relation with the divine, the spiritual, and the eternal, is to individualize infinite power; and this is Christian Science" (*The First Church of Christ, Scientist, and Miscellany*, p. 160).

That explanation, to me, is a living prayer. And isn't this what Jesus did? Didn't he "live so as to keep human consciousness in constant relation with the divine"? Recall the occasion when he had come to raise Lazarus from death. Before he called Lazarus forth, Jesus said: "Father, I thank thee that thou hast heard me. And I knew that thou hearest me always" (John 11:41, 42). *Always*, Jesus said. The Master was certainly living with "consciousness in constant relation with the divine," and thereby God heard him always. The power of divine grace was dramatically witnessed as Lazarus came forth from the tomb still wrapped in his burial shroud. Can you imagine what it must have been like to be standing there and to have witnessed this supreme moment of God's grace in action?

I think it's only by the grace of God that we could ever hope to live as Jesus did, knowing that God hears us always. And to have a certainty of God's ever-present response to our prayers is vital to the practice of Christian healing.

Grace and healing

As God's grace, the influence of His love on our heart, is felt, it is naturally expressed in our experience through the practice of Christianly scientific healing. And healing, in its broadest sense, really points to the final elimination of every vestige of mortality and its corresponding limitations. Such healing means overcoming illness and pain, despair, immorality, poverty, hopelessness, fear, violence, and so on—all of the debilitating lies that confront humanity. Each falsehood, and whatever appears to be its effects in human life, can be eliminated by understanding the true nature of God and of man as His pure, spiritual manifestation. This includes the healing of what might be classified as incurable disease or obdurate sin. And of such healing Mrs. Eddy explained, "All this is accomplished by the grace of God,—the effect of God *understood*" (*Christian Science versus Pantheism*, p. 10).

Mary Baker Eddy clearly linked grace to healing. In one of her letters to a student, Frank Gale, she counseled him about his own healing ministry. In part, she said: "The healing will grow more easy and be more immediate as you realize that God, Good, *is all* and Good is *Love*. You must gain Love, and lose the false sense called love. You must feel the Love that *never faileth*,—that perfect sense of divine power that makes healing no longer power but *grace*. Then you will have the Love that casts out fear and when fear is gone doubt is gone and your work is done. Why? Because it never was *undone*." (L08565, Mary Baker Eddy to Frank Gale, June 9, 1891, The Mary Baker Eddy Collection, The Mary Baker Eddy Library for the Betterment of Humanity.)

In Christian Science healing, there's a demand to relinquish any suggestion that healing is somehow a personal "power" that we possess through a special talent or that we can acquire through mere human means and effort. Instead, we need to be willing to yield unreservedly to divine Love's grace in our healing work. So much of genuine healing is simply the outward evidence of God's grace pouring forth into human lives.

And isn't every instance of healing through prayer, every outward manifestation of God's grace, actually a demonstration of Truth destroying those material elements of thought that obscure our innate harmony? Fundamental to Christian healing is the overcoming of ignorance and fear, yielding up of human will, giving up false trusts, letting go of limited concepts, turning out and eradicating sin whenever necessary. Such transformation in thinking results in the appropriate adjustment of whatever condition may need correcting. It results in healing.

This is what Love's grace accomplishes in us. The action of God's love purifies us of sick, sinful, and limited misconceptions. The divine Love that extracts error and annihilates evil is powerful Love; it can remove whole mountains of false belief from one's thinking. Love's embrace, through the activity of Christ (the divine influence in human thought), brings us out of darkness into the light of Truth. God's grace frees us to be who we really are—the sinless, whole, rejoicing children of God, the spiritual reflection of Life, Truth, and Love. There is no greater joy than discovering how Love constantly cares for each of us—how Love *graces* each of our lives.

In the Old Testament, there is the account of the Shunammite woman whose son had died, and she had gone to the prophet Elisha for help. Her response was central to the healing. When Elisha's servant met her on the way, he asked: "Is it well with thee?" Her immediate reply, even though her son had died, remains a remarkable testament to divine grace: "It is well" (II Kings 4:26). It could only be through grace that in the very midst of some tremendous challenge, when the question comes: "Is it well with us?" that we, too, could humbly and honestly reply, "It *is* well."

This standpoint can be a keynote for our practice of Christian Science healing. The insistent suggestions of what the Apostle Paul calls the carnal mind that something *isn't* well, that something is far from well, that it can't possibly *be* well, can be forthrightly challenged. The insistent suggestions that question our wellness, our wholeness, our relation to God—that impose sick beliefs and symptoms of pain; that deny the presence of God and claim instead that we are limited, weak, and fragile mortals predisposed to illness—all of this can be met with the expectant affirmation, *"It is well!"*

In truth, whatever we confront is *always* well, because we are each the pure and perfect likenesses of our Creator, who is always well. The perfect goodness and wholeness of God is forever reflected in His good and whole children—you and me. We are God's beloved son and daughter "in whom [He is] well pleased" (see Matt. 3:17).

All the good that comes to our lives through grace—all the healing, all the spiritual progress—bears witness not only to the fact that God's love for us surely does abound, but to the reality that the power of His saving Christ is unsurpassed. In *Science and Health*, Mrs. Eddy wrote at length about the great works Jesus performed and how he accomplished all that he did. She concluded one paragraph by affirming, "Grace and Truth are potent beyond all other means and methods" (p. 67). We can take tremendous hope from that realization. We can rejoice in it. We can trust the supreme power and continuing influence of divine grace in our lives—today.

—*William E. Moody*

GROUP DYNAMICS

⟶⟵

The metaphysics of Christian Science is effective in increasing the quality and efficiency in group action. Business and community enterprises today are so complex that planning and action are initiated and carried out by groups of specialists. A team of experts, a committee, or a corporation usually replaces one-man enterprise. And compromise and conservatism as often replace unity and boldness.

Social science analyzes group dynamics and suggests human methods, sometimes helpful, always limited to human conceptions. Christian Science presents a spiritual method. According to this Science, reality and the laws which control it are spiritual, created by one Mind, God; they are absolute. As the individual scientifically applies the absolute truth to his human situation, his understanding and character are transformed. His experience then begins to pattern the harmony and law of divine reality.

As one member of a group changes, all relationships to that member are forced to change, and therefore the entire group changes. And so as one member of the group understands the spiritual reality of demand, ideas, and action, he can use this truth to help the entire group bring out better results. Spiritual understanding of Truth, Mind, and Love demonstrates specific laws of God, for Truth, Mind, and Love are synonymous with God. To the extent that initiative, plan, and work are based on spiritual laws, they are intelligent, efficient, and free from the stifling conflicts of human personalities.

I applied the three dicta outlined later in this article for the first time while I was serving on a committee with a chairman possessed by a desire to appear successful to his superiors. His meticulous assignments and persistent guidance in carrying them out seemed helpful; but I soon saw that this method stifled experiment. He felt strongly about everything and referred to us as "my committee." As the committee shaped its final recommendations, an undercurrent of irritation broke into rivalry. I considered resigning.

It came to me to analyze the problem in the light of Christian Science first. In my prayerful metaphysical realization I did not seek to influence the thoughts of others. In the discussion I made my points conform to what I knew to be spiritually true, and the effect was to lessen the discords and bring out the truly inspired work of the committee. A more productive atmosphere set in; the reports were less structured, and some new plans were presented. I decided to stay.

In my application of Christian Science metaphysics, I saw clearly that Truth makes the demand, Mind produces the ideas, and Love impels the work.

In all types of group activity one needs to question, "What is making the demand: an opportunity, a problem, an executive, a clique?" Mrs. Eddy writes in *Science and Health* (p. 184), "Truth, Life, and Love are the only legitimate and eternal demands on man, and they are spiritual lawgivers, enforcing obedience through divine statutes."

Truth makes the demand. Whether the demand appears as a problem to be solved or as an opportunity to be capitalized, Truth is demanding the demonstration of law, a law of spiritual reality. Therefore the real initiator is Truth. Perhaps Truth is demanding a demonstration of the law of justice or of supply, or is demanding a demonstration of health or of progress or of the law governing relationships. According to Christian Science, the laws governing all reality and activity are spiritual. And Truth has the power to enforce obedience.

The demand may appear discomforting to the human mind and be misinterpreted as a human pressure producing personal responses of reaction, resentment, and resistance to change. If it is understood, however, that Truth's demand initiates the group's work, there will be less personal defensiveness, emotional reaction, rivalry, or fear to interfere with the formulation of workable plans by the members; and group efficiency will be greatly increased.

Individual reliability is expressed spontaneously when the group effort is seen as taking place in the vibrant, healthy atmosphere of Truth's demanding. Here the individual feels trusted and valued. Discerning the infinite but legitimate demand of Truth, he humbly reaches for resources outside himself. He begins to find the spiritual resources of his own true individuality reflecting infinite God. He experiences the thrill of functioning in a state of thought beyond his ordinary human capacity. For Truth's demands are not small. They call for the highest expressions of trustworthiness, fearless morality, inspired logic, intelligence, and skill. These qualities are best expressed by the member who most clearly understands that his true individuality reflects God's absolute perfection.

Truth, the Lawgiver, demands and produces harmony and freedom. Man-made methods and rules are insufficient to enforce obedience. Where spiritual law, not person, is felt to govern a group, dictatorial leadership does not occur. Any required discipline exercised under Truth's demand for harmony and freedom is loving, impersonal; and members accede readily.

Not only are these demands legitimate, but they are eternal, that is, timeless. As one realizes this, the group members are freed from the false sense of time and pressure which would force short-range solutions. The demands of Truth are insistent but without time limits.

If a human problem is accepted as the demand, solutions and plans will be limited by the confines of the problem. Problems do not outline their solutions. By turning to God, the one universal Mind, thought becomes occupied with totally different, often radically new, means which take the solution great strides beyond a single step forward. What can fulfill an infinite demand? Only infinite Mind, God. Truth makes the demand. Mind produces the ideas. Mind knows what Truth is demanding.

Interpreting the Genesis account of God's creating of the stars and of the two great lights to rule the day and the night, Mrs. Eddy states (*Science and Health*, pp. 510–511): "Science reveals only one Mind, and this one shining by its own light and governing the universe, including man, in perfect harmony. This Mind forms ideas, its own images, subdivides and radiates their borrowed light, intelligence, and so explains the Scripture phrase, 'whose seed is in itself.'"

What a clear explanation of God's method of creation! Ideas formed by one Mind! They are not produced by bouncing one idea off another. They do not spawn each other. They do not conflict. One Mind alone produces them. Mind's ideas are complete and perfect needing no revision. They reflect beauty and order; and their unfolding is perfect. Infinite Mind has an inexhaustible supply of ideas. Their radiating intelligence attracts, and no coercion is necessary to persuade.

Those who demonstrate these spiritual ideas will formulate human plans which are bold, complete, and beautiful. The expression itself, graphic, oral, or delineated in another way, will develop naturally, as does the spiritual idea from the seed within itself. Such human plans, expressing intelligence and art, accomplish their purposes. No long testing periods of trial and error will be needed to prove them out.

A human plan based on Mind's ideas is fearlessly moral. It never requires an ethical compromise, although human compromise may appear in the process of working out such a plan. When it has been worked out from a spiritual basis, intelligence and fairness bring justice to all. No one can be harmed, and no good can be displaced by a plan patterned after Mind's ideas. Mortal mind, which attempts to create and possess ideas, must be discarded. Its personal suggestions are crude, exhaustible, lacking scope and brilliance.

To distinguish a plan based on Mind's ideas, from a plan based on personal suggestions, we must discern the original which each patterns. Does it pattern the purpose and intelligence of a divine idea, or is it patterned merely on personal desire and materialistic reasoning? Intelligently worked-out plans work out intelligently. Talk has not produced them. And plans that are not produced by talk cannot remain in a talking stage. They are carried out.

Speaking of God as Love, Mrs. Eddy says in *Miscellaneous Writings* (p. 358), "Love impels good works." Divine Love is the tender persuader motivating the real man and causing him to act according to Mind's purpose. This is a law of Love. Even one member of the group applying the power of Love according to the metaphysical method of Christian Science will help to destroy friction and demonstrate the spiritual laws governing action. He loves his fellow workers; he loves himself in a true spiritual sense; he loves his work.

All that can be accomplished must be done through the quiet catalytic power of love. Greatly loved tasks are done with effortless freedom. Neither time, nor muscle, nor calculation inhibits. True love inspires, coordinates, and speeds group work. Every member becomes an ergophile. How right Paul was when he wrote (Gal. 5:6), "In Jesus Christ neither circumcision availeth any thing, nor uncircumcision; but faith which worketh by love"!

Whoever expresses the "faith which worketh by love" expedites action and benefits the group, whether that group is a family, a committee, or a corporation. The Love which gave Moses the Ten Commandments blessed a nation (Ex. 18:13–27). The Love through which Christ Jesus healed the nobleman's son also converted a whole household (see John 4:45–53). The Love which revealed Christian Science to Mrs. Eddy gave her consummate skill in dealing with the press, the courts, her church, and audiences of thousands.

Truth makes the demand, Mind produces the ideas, and Love impels the work.

—*Mary Gertrude Bayless*

THE HOLY GHOST AND HEALING

∽

To those engaged in the practice of Christian healing, Mary Baker Eddy offers this encouragement and instruction: "Hold perpetually this thought,—that it is the spiritual idea, the Holy Ghost and Christ, which enables you to demonstrate, with scientific certainty, the rule of healing, based upon its divine Principle, Love, underlying, overlying, and encompassing all true being" (*Science and Health*, p. 496). The Holy Ghost and Christ. For many, *Christ* is a familiar term, but what is the Holy Ghost, and how does it aid in the healing work?

Christian Science teaches that the Holy Ghost is synonymous with divine Science, the Comforter promised by Christ Jesus. It is the full revelation of Truth, making known the deepest things of God and the spiritual import of the life of His Son, Christ Jesus. Jesus' life revealed the depth, height, breadth, and power of divine Love. The Holy Ghost reveals Love to be immortal and omnipresent, the ever-operative Principle. It presents man as the work of Love, living in the realm of Love, under the rule of Love—as God's perfect, constant reflection. In the Glossary of *Science and Health*, Mrs. Eddy provides the spiritual meaning of *Holy Ghost:* "Divine Science; the development of eternal Life, Truth, and Love" (p. 588). This Science is vital—a living power. It operates universally, without boundaries. It unfolds the healing power of true Christianity.

Divine Science presents the entire glory of God. In Science, God is never seen apart from His manifestation, for Principle and idea, God and man, are one in being. Jesus was conscious of his divine relation to God. He prayed, "And now, O Father, glorify thou me with thine own self with the glory which I had with thee before the world was" (John 17:5). Man's real selfhood, as presented by Christ, has never been separated from God, but abides eternally with our Father as His image and likeness. Divine Science reminds us how Christ destroys the belief of an Adam-like man, of a man separate from and independent of his creator. Man is the direct outcome of God, the outcome of the activity of Truth, of Life, of Spirit. Can the outcome of Truth be error? Can the outcome of Life be death? Can the outcome of Spirit be a sinning mortal?

Never. God is the living Principle, the perpetual cause or author of all being. Man's identity, essence, and nature are found in Him and are of God alone. The Holy Ghost reveals man reflecting all the glory of God.

When Jesus was baptized by John, "the heaven was opened, and the Holy Ghost descended in a bodily shape like a dove upon him...." (Luke 3:21, 22.) Submerged in the recognition of the allness of Spirit, Jesus was filled with the Holy Ghost, the understanding of divine Science. Then his pure and sinless nature heard the voice of God identifying him as His beloved Son. In proportion as we are touched by the Holy Ghost, our own lives are purified and we become conscious of God's knowledge of us as His beloved sons and daughters. This spiritual sense governs us, and being conscious of man's unity with God, the only Ego, we are freed from the material sense of illness and pain.

Every Christian Science Sunday service is designed to rouse mankind to feel the presence and power of the Holy Ghost. The service is capped by "the scientific statement of being" from *Science and Health* (see *Science and Health*, p. 468) and this correlative scripture from First John: "Behold, what manner of love the Father hath bestowed upon us, that we should be called the sons of God: therefore the world knoweth us not, because it knew him not. Beloved, now are we the sons of God, and it doth not appear what we shall be: but we know that, when he shall appear, we shall be like him; for we shall see him as he is. And every man that hath this hope in him purifieth himself, even as he is pure" (I John 3:1–3). As this "dove" descends upon the congregation, man in the likeness of Love is more clearly revealed and the healing power of Christ made known.

John the Baptist told those who came to be baptized in the river Jordan that Jesus, when he came, would baptize with the Holy Ghost and fire. Mrs. Eddy writes in *Science and Health* that Science "brings the baptism of the Holy Ghost, whose flames of Truth were prophetically described by John the Baptist as consuming error" (*Science and Health*, p. 558). Baptism in water sounds all right to most, but baptism by fire may give some pause.

It's helpful to note the difference between the flames of hell, and the flames of Truth. The flames of hell are punishing and torturous. They are composed of guilt, anger, vengeance, pain, lust, hatred, and grief. These constitute sin's own self-destructive nature. Here or hereafter, either sin's self-torment or a growing understanding of divine Science causes mortals to retreat from their association with sin. Like the prodigal son in Jesus' parable, they come to their senses, remember their true Father, and return to His presence.

The flames of Truth are cleansing and purifying. They refine the substance of thought and bring out the gold in character. The gold is not destroyed, it is purified; only the dross, the errors of sense, is consumed. The account of Shadrach, Meshach, and Abednego in the Old Testament is illustrative. (See Dan., chap. 3.) They were not harmed or burned or caused to suffer in any way in the king's furnace. Only the ropes that bound them burned. When the king looked into the fiery furnace, he saw a fourth man walking with them who had the appearance of the Son of God. The Holy Ghost revealed the true nature and substance of man—spiritual, indestructible, and immortal. Today, the "ropes," or beliefs in disease, that attempt to bind mankind are burned by the flames of Truth. Again, the Science of man—that he is not material, but spiritual—is revealed.

In her essay "Pond and Purpose" Mrs. Eddy explains, "The baptism of the Holy Ghost is the spirit of Truth cleansing from all sin; giving mortals new motives, new purposes, new affections, all pointing upward" (*Miscellaneous Writings*, p. 204). The revelation of Truth is not an intellectual or philosophical ideal suitable only for contemplation. It expresses the divine energy of Spirit quickening and energizing its ideas. The Holy Ghost transforms our lives. Healed of sickness and delivered from sin, we recognize that divine Science has given us a new heart, and we long to see more of the new heaven and new earth prophesied by St. John. Science is the leaven spoken of in one of Jesus' parables; it was revealed by God to Mrs. Eddy and is contained in her work *Science and Health with Key to the Scriptures*.

The carnal mind's hatred of Truth is often evidenced in its hatred of the woman, Mary Baker Eddy, by whom Truth has reached and blessed our age. Its efforts to impugn the character and credibility of God's scribe are designed to hide the evidence of the Holy Ghost and its healing power from mankind. Contention regarding the Discoverer of Christian Science is animal magnetism's means of blinding mankind to the glory of Truth's revelation. But the flames of Truth are more than sufficient to burn the dross—every machination of the carnal mind. The Holy Ghost eternally unfolds the saving

power of God as presented in divine Science—it is a light that cannot be darkened. And it is in this light that we can discern the true character of our Leader.

Mrs. Eddy writes in *Science and Health* (p. 107) that God had prepared her to receive the revelation of divine Science. From her earliest years her character was tried and refined by Spirit. She had a natural affinity for Spirit, an abiding love for God's Word. An unselfed love was a special mark of her nature from earliest childhood. Though she grew up in the atmosphere of Calvinism, which often spoke more vigorously of the certain punishment of man than of his salvation, her heart naturally gravitated to a God who presented Himself to her as eternal and universal Love. It was the consciousness of God's love rather than a belief in His sternness that healed her of a bad fever (see *Retrospection and Introspection* by Mrs. Eddy, p. 13) and later enabled her to heal a blind child through prayer years before her discovery of Christian Science (Church History document: A10402).

These kinds of events increased her hunger to understand God and the healing power of Christ. Yet the doctrine of dispensationalism, the theory that limits the healing works of Jesus to his own day, prevailed in her time as it often does in ours. So, experiencing frequent and painful invalidism, and unhelped by the common practice of medicine, she sought out the alternative health systems of her day, as we see so many doing today. But during all this time she never ceased to live a God-centered, Bible-centered experience. Spirit was the central axis of her life. Severe illness, the sudden death of her first husband, the death of her parents, being deprived of her child, severe poverty, the infidelity of her second husband, continued ill health—not one of these shook her constant resort to God. She was tested and tried and persistently proven faithful.

No one else was prepared to receive the revelation of divine Science; no one else endured the preparation of Truth, Life, and Love for this purpose. The uniqueness of her character, the degree to which her own nature was refined by the flames of Truth, can be seen in contrast to the frailty of those who thought they could take over her work. One early promising student proved unable to meet the assault of sensualism. He deserted her and then turned against her. Her adopted son found the allure of society and travel more satisfying than the rigid discipline of divine Science. One of her publishers was unable to accept a woman's leadership, the superiority of spiritual sense over untempered business know-how, and he deserted the Cause. Several prominent students failed to quench the desire for personal power and prestige and proved unable to submit to the demands of Truth and Love. In Mrs. Eddy, purity, discipline, humility, spiritual strength, steadfastness, fidelity, grace, and love combined to form a character truly receptive and obedient to Truth. Her life cannot be separated from the truth she served.

Driving through New Hampshire, one can look at the same mountains that Mrs. Eddy often saw during her early years. As one learns to appreciate her work, one has to conclude that she had a spiritual core that was stronger than these mountains and that her work will outlast them all.

Jesus declared that the Comforter, or Holy Ghost, would be with us forever. Nothing can turn back the revelation of divine Science nor negate the power of God's Word. It reveals the unalterable Principle of all being.

Have you considered the self-revealing power of God's Word breaking through human ignorance—even hate; the might and purpose of divine Love as manifested in the life of Christ Jesus and in the teachings of the Holy Ghost? The divine power that impelled such momentous spiritual breakthroughs is the same power that backs the practice of Christian healing. Knowledge of this gives one "scientific certainty" in the practice of Christian Science. The Holy Ghost and Christ bring us before the throne of God, the might and glory of divine Love.

—*Richard C. Bergenheim*

"IMMORTAL MIND ... SUPREME IN THE PHYSICAL REALM"

When I was a young student of Christian Science, I had difficulty in harmonizing Mrs. Eddy's "scientific statement of being"—including its declaration that "there is no life, truth, intelligence, nor substance in matter" (*Science and Health*, p. 468)—with another of her statements, "Immortal Mind, governing all, must be acknowledged as supreme in the physical realm, so-called, as well as in the spiritual" (p. 427). I was puzzled how to apply to physical problems a Science that denies the existence of matter.

The question was answered for me in another of Mrs. Eddy's statements: "Metaphysics resolves things into thoughts, and exchanges the objects of sense for the ideas of Soul" (*Science and Health*, p. 269). I began to realize that even in the physical realm all things are actually thoughts. Good thoughts are derived from divine Principle, Mind, and evil thoughts have no life, substance, or intelligence.

The statement 2 + 2 = 3 has no part or place in our normal number system, yet it is subject to the correcting aspect of that system. The statement does involve valid quantities, but because their relationship is not according to fact, we have here a statement of what is *not true* about the quantities involved. In music, consecutive fifths are no part of a normal four-part chorale, and yet that mistake is subject to the rules governing this musical form.

In like manner, the elements or parts of the human anatomy are all thoughts. Disarrangement and symptoms of disease are no part of the divine Principle, which governs the body. Still, they do come under the correcting aspect of the divine law. Sin, disease, and death are no more natural to man than errors are a part of music or arithmetic.

This point is a great help in learning how to apply absolute Christian Science to physical problems. Understanding the divine control of infinite Mind and the mental nature of the human anatomy is not only useful in healing the sick but in all activities involving the human body, such as art, dance, athletics, marriage, etc. The jurisdiction of divine Mind, Love, has the effect of sustaining those human thoughts which rightfully symbolize and represent spiritual concepts, qualities, and functions—and dissolving those human thoughts which do not represent the presence of God, good, and are therefore erroneous.

This approach can be carried further. If metaphysics resolves *all* things into thoughts, then people are thoughts and places are thoughts. Dollars, pounds and pence, francs—all thoughts. Stock markets, businesses, unions, conglomerates, and churches—all are compound thoughts.

What is the relationship between these thoughts and man? The real man is the expression, the reflection, of the divine Mind. Therefore he reflects the jurisdiction that the divine Mind, or Ego, has over all thoughts. This is how individual man has dominion over the earth: by reflecting the infinite power of the all-knowing Mind over its ideas. When the human being reflects in his thinking the truth that life, substance, and intelligence are spiritual and good, his experience reflects in terms of human things and thoughts the natural harmony, health, affluence, strength, and intelligence of his original spiritual being.

The practice of Christian Science takes the concepts of Spirit and the qualities of divine Love and embraces all the complex thoughts confronting humankind, including those that are political, economic, financial, and social. This is how the individual Christian Scientist can, through his prayer, have an influence in world affairs. When we give up our human sense of ego, realize to some degree the oneness of infinite, divine Mind, and humbly seek to reflect the will and action of this Mind, we find that we reflect vast mental influence and power for good in world affairs. This is how the meek can inherit the earth.

When a personal sense of ego tries to inherit or dominate the material earth, it becomes tyrannical and greedy, and may be expressed by dictatorship. Personal sense would conquer the world by subduing persons and nations. But when the Christ, as the manifestation of divine, intelligent Mind, embraces our sense of creation, we let God's will be done and have full faith in His spiritual disposal of events. Spiritual sense does not subdue persons and nations but does subdue the belief in a self-created and self-acting physical universe. The scientific Christian becomes a world conqueror by letting

Truth and Love dominate his beliefs about the world, and by letting godliness, or his Christ nature, animate his motives and efforts. He conquers the personal sense of self through realizing the divine Mind, the infinite Ego, as his Mind.

This prayer is not a generalized affirmation of abstract good. Christian Science prayer treats specific thoughts and brings them under the corrective jurisdiction of divine Truth, the Christ-principle. That is one reason why, in Christian Science, the prayer that heals is called Christian Science treatment.

As we exercise this prayerful, powerful, individual influence in world affairs, it is important to understand these points: that the concept of a personal ego is erroneous; that all men have one infinite, divine Mind; that each individual is, in his real being, a spiritual reflection—a conscious identity—in this Mind; and that *all* human thought, be it legitimate or erroneous, comes under the jurisdiction of this Mind, ruling out errors and unfolding Mind's own manifestation and individual expression.

The application of these truths to specific problems will render error powerless and bring out the power and effect of Christ in human affairs. War, organized crime, epidemics, famine, the contagion of animality and sympathetic sin, are statements of what is *not true* about life, man, being, relationship, and so on.

So even matter and error are subject to the correcting presence of Mind, divine Principle, because all things, from molecules to mountains, are really thoughts. This understanding makes practical for us Christ Jesus' prayer "Thy will be done in earth, as it is in heaven" (Matt. 6:10) and that of David, "Thine, O Lord, is the greatness, and the power, and the glory, and the victory, and the majesty: for all that is in the heaven and in the earth is thine; thine is the kingdom, O Lord, and thou art exalted as head above all" (I Chron. 29:11).

Christian Science healing is the process of adjusting human beliefs on the basis of the divine jurisdiction so that they conform to true, spiritual facts.

—*Helen C. Moon*

INCURABILITY: A LIE ABOUT LIFE

$\mathcal{W}$hen one awakes to the divine authority by which man lives, he will no longer fear that disease can kill him, and the myth of incurability will be disproved.

In Christian Science one learns that there is no life in matter, for Life is God. Therefore man's individual life, reflecting the divine Life, is an orderly unfoldment of harmonious activity. On the other hand, whatever represents the unintelligent, undisciplined, disintegrating force of disease and death must be ruled out of our understanding of Life, for such so-called action can never proceed from the loving creator.

The belief in incurability stems solely from the false belief that life is in matter instead of in God, Spirit. The label of incurability is placed on certain conditions by a system of healing that mistakenly treats matter as cause and disease as effect. The treatment is as material as the diagnosis, and they combine as an aggressive hoax, a belief enforced by a mortal mind convinced of its own reality. To control the condition of their bodies and produce health, men need to understand that matter is but the subjective state of mortal mind.

Disease seems to operate as a counterforce to divine power, opposing the harmony of man. But an understanding of the law of Life can heal any disease, whether or not it is labeled incurable, by depriving it of any claim to power and force. Referring to material forces in general, Mrs. Eddy says, "The material so-called gases and forces are counterfeits of the spiritual forces of divine Mind, whose potency is Truth, whose attraction is Love, whose adhesion and cohesion are Life, perpetuating the eternal facts of being" (*Science and Health*, p. 293).

To understand the perpetuating power of eternal Life, and to express the life-giving qualities of the divine nature, enables one to bring into his experience all that is necessary for harmonious existence. The very force of Life is uniting and holding together all the elements of Life. This divine power cannot be set aside or split asunder by so-called counterforces of disease and death.

To perpetuate the facts of being in our experience through understanding the adhesive, cohesive forces of Life is to deprive mortal mind, alias matter, of a foothold. The law of divine Mind, when applied, holds together what belongs together in our experience. And through the unifying force of Life it just as surely separates and destroys whatever is foreign to Life and its expression. Disease, being strictly material, shares no common ground with Spirit. Matter and its conditions have no place in the realm of Truth. Thus one finds his exemption from any form of discordant matter when he sees that the discord has no adhesive, cohesive force.

Deteriorating disease is a belief that mankind can suffer from a lack of the forces of Life such as strength, purity, and free-flowing action. The physical body, being the expression of mortal thought, responds to this false belief and finds itself succumbing to a supposition called malfunctioning matter. Unless this discord is halted through divine Mind's action, understood and affirmed, the belief in death claims to blot out one's existence. But Mind's control over man and the universe is an established spiritual fact that lays bare the lie of life in matter.

Matter never gave man life, nor can it deprive him of it. God, being all-acting, is responsible for all the activities of His creation. Man does not originate action but reflects it, and his existence is dependent solely on divine Life. Therefore the activities of Life cannot be interrupted through the destruction of its expression, man. To destroy God's creation, one would have to destroy God. What we need comes to us directly from God, from the source of Life itself. Strength, purity, and vitality are divine attributes, and always available to us through an understanding of the Christ, our perfect relationship to God. Divine Mind imparts these life-saving qualities, and the forces of adhesion and cohesion inherent in Spirit hold man forever intact as a reflection of the power of Life.

Whenever the false law of disease claims to deprive one of what is essential to harmonious being, the power of Life, when understood, acts as a restorative force. The perpetuating facts of eternal being are always operating to hold us perfectly in Life and to destroy the fear of disease and death. But we need to be receptive of these divine facts and to hold to them.

The belief of incurability also seems to work in another direction. Instead of deterioration, it sometimes produces runaway action in the form of abnormal growth. In such cases the same spiritual law of the adhesion and cohesion of Life, when affirmed, can eliminate the growth, for surely the law of Life that unites what belongs together is just as effective in separating what does *not* belong together.

True growth is a divine activity. It is a spiritually mental state governed solely by divine Principle. God could never authorize an activity to destroy His creation. Whatever appears as diseased growth can really be classified as non-growth, for it is a manifestation of wrong states of thought. Sometimes it represents such undisciplined and ungodlike thinking as resentment, fear, guilt, sorrow, or anger. At times it even represents an intense self-will that will not be bridled. Divine Love is not expressed by such thoughts. We express Love's will for man when we are truly loving, and thereby we overcome willful thinking and action. Thus we understand how both evil thought and its manifestations were never a part of God's creation.

Mrs. Eddy sets up the criteria for true growth when she writes in *Miscellaneous Writings*, "Growth is governed by intelligence; by the active, all-wise, law-creating, law-disciplining, law-abiding Principle, God" (p. 206).

In the book of Hebrews we find the operation of the great law of Life suggested in this way: "The word of God is quick, and powerful, and sharper than any two edged sword, piercing even to the dividing asunder of soul and spirit, and of the joints and marrow, and is a discerner of the thoughts and intents of the heart" (4:12). This verse can be likened to Christian Science treatment, which both denies the error and affirms the truth. It takes both edges of the sword of Truth to penetrate and destroy the evils of sin, disease, and death and so perpetuate the spiritual facts of eternal being.

Jesus did not bow to the lie of incurability or death. He raised the dead on several occasions as well as restoring himself, unchanged, after three days in the grave. His understanding of the laws of Life proved forever to all mankind the blatant error of belief in the inevitability of death. This great fact, understood, should close the book forever on the belief that there is any incurable situation.

—Joanne Shriver Leedom

INDIVIDUALITY—ITS ETERNAL PRESENCE

Some people who have lost loved ones have been deeply comforted—and even healed of grief—through realizing that every precious quality they cherished in their loved ones, they also, as children of God, fully and beautifully express. After all, each of God's sons and daughters reflects the wholeness of His nature, right here and now.

Yet in the midst of grief, even a recognition of this profound truth sometimes leaves people feeling that something is missing. And most people, if you asked them, would probably tell you that their suffering comes from the absence of their loved one; that the expression of the same spiritual God qualities in themselves and others—tenderness, humor, unselfishness, for example—simply doesn't substitute for that loved one's specific presence. But then, how could it? Identity isn't merely generic; it is marvelously and exquisitely *individual*. Individuality is the glorious *art* of our being, the original way in which each one of us expresses the universal spiritual qualities of God. In fact, because God is the incomparable One, all that He creates must reflect that oneness, must be incomparably, irreplaceably individual. In the Christian Science textbook, *Science and Health with Key to the Scriptures*, Mary Baker Eddy explains, "The one Ego, the one Mind or Spirit called God, is infinite individuality, which supplies all form and comeliness and which reflects reality and divinity in individual spiritual man and things" (p. 281).

What we actually love, and what we seem to miss when someone we hold dear passes from our sight, is that loved one's completely individual way of expressing the qualities of God. So what we may need to recognize when we are dealing with grief is the breathtaking truth of the specific *presence* of individuality.

The fact is that even when we're certain that our loved one is continuing on, we seem to be equally certain that this continuity does not mean distinct individual presence here and now. Yet how could this be so when "here" and "hereafter" there is only one Life. And since the one all-inclusive, omnipresent Life is continuously with us, how could Life's entire manifestation not be continuously with us—all of the individualities that are eternally inseparable from the Life and Mind conceiving them? How could there possibly be absence in omnipresence?

What confuses the issue is the mistaken belief that matter is connected to, and is the medium of, someone's presence; that without matter, nothing would have form or means of expression. This is the fundamental error that causes us to lose sight of our loved ones. Understanding that life isn't defined or determined by matter, Jesus was able to raise people from the dead, and *Science and Health* says, "When you can waken yourself or others out of the belief that all must die, you can then exercise Jesus' spiritual power to reproduce the presence of those who have thought they died,—but not otherwise" (p. 75).

The spiritual origin, perpetual presence, and eternal continuity of life was demonstrated in its fullness through the virgin conception, life, works, crucifixion, resurrection, and ascension of Christ Jesus. His own perfect life, as well as his consistent, extraordinary healing work, brought to light the image of God, proving men and women to be in their true nature, Godlike. In fact, through his many healings, Jesus showed us the present reality of true, spiritual individuality. An individuality that exists before the belief of material conception and birth. An individuality that is visible to spiritual sense.

Through his example, we discover that it is only to darkened, earthbound thought that spiritual individuality is invisible. Jesus saw God's flawless likeness everywhere—the individual whose Father and Mother is the divine Principle, Love. And he saw that flawless individuality in the very place where the material senses saw a material personality. *Science and Health* explains: "Jesus beheld in Science the perfect man, who appeared to him where sinning mortal man appears to mortals. In this perfect man the Saviour saw God's own likeness, and this correct view of man healed the sick" (pp. 476–477).

A number of years ago, a woman realized that her deepest desire and most earnest prayer to God was to understand what it means to see "in Science the perfect man" right here on earth, as Jesus did. She felt that this was the quintessence of Christian Science practice. Within that following year, her husband passed on. A few days afterward, in the middle of a sleepless night, she sat up and reached out to God with all her heart, asking specifically for a glimpse of what it means to behold "in Science the perfect man." Immediately, it was as though the room was filled with light, and a penetrating, all-embracing love. Enveloped in this love, she felt her husband's presence, and clearly discerned his specific spiritual individuality. She wasn't seeing the spirit of someone who had departed, nor was she communicating with a spirit. Rather, she was seeing his identity from a higher standpoint—"in Science"—which defined and revealed her husband with a crystal clarity unbound by the veil of material sense. It was a knowledge of who he was beyond any she had ever had before.

A few months after this experience, she received a telephone call telling her that a dear friend had been in a serious automobile accident and was in the hospital. Many weeks later, she was told that although her friend's eyes were open, she had not "awakened"—that is, she did not appear to have any awareness of herself, of others, or of her surroundings. It was believed that this "awakening" would have to occur in order for her friend to recover. The woman set out to visit this friend in the hospital, and because of the experience she had had after her husband's passing, she was absolutely certain that she would see through the belief that matter constituted this friend's individual presence and consciousness. In fact, when she entered the hospital room, she felt that same light of divine Love revealing her friend's conscious individuality. She looked at her and addressed her, certain that her friend would know her and respond. She did, and this was the turning point in her friend's complete recovery.

The true nature of individuality is visible to spiritual sense here and now as idea, not as matter or material personality. And if we believe that there is something vague or intangible about spiritual individuality, we need only look again to the experience of our Lord: Jesus talked with Moses and Elias on the mount of transfiguration. (See Matt. 17:1–8.) This wasn't spiritualism—belief in communication with departed spirits. It was beholding "in Science the perfect man" that enabled the inspired meeting—beholding the individual whose presence then and now, on earth as in heaven, is not dependent on matter, and can never be made to suffer the confinement of time and space.

In response to the question "What is man?" *Science and Health* gives this revolutionary definition: "Man is idea, the image, of Love; he is not physique. He is the compound idea of God, including all right ideas…" (p. 475). Perhaps we've seen right

ideas as those constructive ideas meeting our needs moment by moment; or as faculties and functions like sight, memory, and digestion.

But in *Science and Health*, *ideas* most often refer to the individual forms, identities, and entities in creation. The stars and planets, the mountains, rocks, trees, flowers, grains of sand, blades of grass, all creatures, men and women—these are, in their true nature, ideas, and as such are permanent, indestructible. *Science and Health* says, "The divine Mind maintains all identities, from a blade of grass to a star, as distinct and eternal" (p. 70). Then each one of us, reflecting infinite, all-inclusive Mind, must include "all right ideas." We must be conscious of and appreciate each individual who ever was, is now, or ever will be in the eternal unfolding of spiritual being. So when a loved one passes from our sight, we not only continue to include his or her lovely qualities, we continue to include the loved one as well. That is, we can feel and recognize the presence of an individual in our consciousness. And we can progressively appreciate his or her specific individuality. Still, one might well ask how we do this.

Almost everybody learns in grade school that even though all snowflakes have a common recognizable identity, or classification, no two snowflakes are alike. What makes them different? *Composition*—the way the elements that constitute a snowflake are arranged, the relationship of the snowflake bits to one another. And perhaps it seems all too obvious to say that every composer of music consistently sounds like himself or herself, no matter how many hundreds of pieces he or she composes; and that we are able to consistently distinguish one composer from another, even though all are using the same notes and expressing through these notes the same universal qualities. But why this individual consistency of sound or style? What produces it? It is the way the notes are composed. Or in other words, the *relationship* of the notes to one another—a relationship forming a unique structure, an individual harmonic pattern, that, although capable of infinite variation and eternal development, remains mathematically constant, forever identifying one individual.

To mortal thought, composition, or arrangement, is always some form of organized matter, in which structure results from the action of physical forces, or laws. And it is symbolized by the man created from dust in the second chapter of Genesis, or by an updated version that one might call the "atomic dust man" or "DNA man." This mortal personality is described as formed of billions of genetic bits of information that are able to be manipulated, rearranged, and cloned. But is this the basic reality of our being? Every physical healing accomplished through an understanding of spiritual identity not only calls this into question, but proves matter to be an illusion of the material senses, not reality. Material personality only simulates the structure of real individuality, a spiritual structure to which nothing can be added and from which nothing can be removed, nor can any element of it be rearranged, manipulated, or cloned. In the Bible, the book of Ecclesiastes says: ". . . whatsoever God doeth, it shall be for ever: nothing can be put to it, nor any thing taken from it" (Eccl. 3:14).

The true structure, or embodiment, of each one's individuality is completely spiritual and mental. It is a unique unduplicated harmony composed of "all right ideas"—a harmony resulting from the perpetual gathering action of *spiritual* force, the law of the divine Principle, Love. This law of Love both reveals and sustains the structure that is our spiritual individuality. The New Testament refers to this dynamic divine energy as the Holy Ghost, and in her book *Unity of Good*, Mrs. Eddy explains, "This Science of God and man is the Holy Ghost, which reveals and sustains the unbroken and eternal harmony of both God and the universe" (*Unity of Good*, p. 52). Because the individual structure of selfhood is eternally sustained, each one's true individuality—completely separate from matter— is permanent, and perfectly discernible to the consciousness filled with spiritual love. *Science and Health* explains, "Thought will finally be understood and seen in all form, substance, and color, but without material accompaniments" (p. 310).

Our true self, then, is "idea, the image, of Love" and not physique. Our specifically "shaped," precisely and harmoniously composed individual consciousness develops and progresses forever. Each one of us is, right now, indestructible, irreplaceable, eternally dear to both God and His children. And nothing about us can ever be lost or changed through willful or accidental disarrangement, or through decomposition. In fact, one of the Messianic prophecies was that God's "Holy One" would never see corruption. (See Ps. 16:10; Acts 2:25–28.) Indeed, Jesus fully demonstrated the incorruptible nature of true structure, or body, in the resurrection and ascension, conclusively illustrating the fact that, even now, in our present experience, identity is not material. It is spiritual. We follow him when we take up the cross as he commanded, and immolate the superficial, personal sense of self that hides our ever-present spiritual individuality, the image of Love.

Many people feel that their appreciation of loved ones who have gone on continues to grow and develop. As we embrace the deepest meanings of individuality and inclusion, we will feel more distinctly our inseparability from absent loved ones. And as this enlightened view is maintained, it must dispel the darkness of loneliness and grief. *Science and Health* reassures us, "Spiritually to understand that there is but one creator, God, unfolds all creation, confirms the Scriptures, brings the sweet assurance of no parting, no pain, and of man deathless and perfect and eternal" (p. 69).

—*Barbara Cook*

LET THE ANGELS TELL THEM

ANGELS. *God's thoughts passing to man; spiritual intuitions, pure and perfect; the inspiration of goodness, purity, and immortality, counteracting all evil, sensuality, and mortality. (Mary Baker Eddy,* Science and Health, *p. 581)*

Isaiah of old said, "Hear now, behold,
a virgin, conceiving, shall bear a son."

Indeed it would be as God's prophet foretold.
But who would tell Mary, the favored one?

Let Gabriel; let the angel tell
Mary, the virgin, of the Highest's will.

Who would tell Joseph and make him believe
that here was a virgin who could so conceive?

The wise virgin Mary let an angel tell him.
(Let an angel tarry, for more surely, we find,
does one believe angels than words from mankind.)

Who was there to go out at nighttime and tell
the shepherds who wandered high up on a hill
that the Saviour was born? It was a bright angel
who brought them good tidings of joy for all people.

Practicing Christians, prepared to convey
the Christ understanding that's with us today,
proclaim the glad tidings.

And should one refuse
to hear healing truths from lips of men,
let the angels,
let the angels,
let the angels tell them.

—*Jane Murdock*

"LET TRUTH UNCOVER...ERROR"

☙

The practice of Christian Science includes the denial of any reality in sin, disease, mortality, and death through understanding the true idea of God as infinite, perfect Mind, and man as His sinless, healthy, harmonious expression. In this healing work some particular phase of habitual wrong thinking in the patient's thought is often uncovered and destroyed, and the healing thereby facilitated.

Sometimes students have, however, overemphasized the need to uncover some specific error in order to accomplish a healing, and have given more attention to uncovering error than to the realization of the spiritual truth of God's allness and man's oneness with Him, the discernment of which confers Truth's healing power. Well-meaning workers have been known to dig deep with the spade of inquisitiveness, or to pry with the chisel of suspicion, into a patient's past. Such an attitude often discourages or frightens the patient, and avails nothing in building up his faith and trust in God and His saving Christ, which is the real purpose of Christian Science practice.

The scientific way is not to be in any wise indifferent to the uncovering of error, but to let the uncovering come in the way of Truth's ordering, and not through a personal inquisition accompanied, perhaps, with personal condemnation. It is right and necessary for an individual to recognize his mistakes and correct them. But to pick out some particular error in his experience and jump to the conclusion that it is, for certain, the one from which subsequent troubles have evolved is a grave mistake. Such human reasoning often leads one sadly awry.

How presumptuous it would be to assume that because a patient gambled on the races, or lost his temper, in 1930, these mistakes resulted in his having rheumatism in 1940! If his derelictions had been more recent and more serious, it would still be a mistake for mere human reasoning to link them unqualifiedly with some present physical difficulty.

Mary Baker Eddy, the Discoverer and Founder of Christian Science, defines the one right course thus: "Let Truth uncover and destroy error in God's own way, and let human justice pattern the divine" (*Science and Health with Key to the Scriptures*, p. 542). Truth and its omniactive, error-exposing forces must be trusted and expected to uncover and destroy any contributing error in God's own way—wisdom's way—not in the human mind's often unwise way.

The healing is God's work to do, and omniscient Mind impels every step to aid in its accomplishment. This fact the Christian Scientist needs often to remember. His work is, through spiritual sense, to realize what God is, and is doing, and man's inherent spiritual oneness with the All-in-all. The understanding of these basic facts operates as a law to free the patient, and to bring to light and destroy every phase of error, be it fear, hate, self-will, or sin, that might claim to be an obstruction to the healing.

The basic error is always mortal mind, and the Christian Scientist should always strike at this error by knowing that since God is the one infinite and immortal Mind, there can be no mortal mind. Its seeming presence is a negation, a fiction. It is of first importance to see that every effect of the basic error, be it sin, sickness, war, death, or a material sense of creation peopled with materially-minded mortals, is as erroneous as the basic error itself. No effect of a false cause can lift itself above the low, truthless level of its cause. Oftentimes when confronted with mortal mind's argument of organization, multiplication, extension, and aggressive mortal mentalities, this important evil-deflating fact is lost sight of. If we unsee the root error, mortal mind, sufficiently with spiritual truth, the remote and immediate cause of the wrong condition is handled.

For every look we take at error, we shall do well to look longer and much oftener to the living Christ. Mrs. Eddy saw, and wished us to see, that it is not by digging in the mire of material beliefs that we find and demonstrate Truth's healing power, but by looking to the redemptive power of eternal Love and man's unity therewith, realizing that it will turn and overturn with the wisdom and thoroughness that no amount of mere human effort can attain.

The Gospels say of Christ Jesus that "he knew their thoughts;" (Luke 6:8) and Mrs. Eddy says on page 95 of *Science and Health*, "We approach God, or Life, in proportion to our spirituality, our fidelity to Truth and Love; and in that ratio we know all human need and are able to discern the thought of the sick and the sinning for the purpose of healing them." Farther on she says, "This kind of mind-reading is not clairvoyance, but it is important to success in healing, and is one of the special characteristics thereof." Here is something for every Christian Scientist to ponder well.

In the ratio of our spirituality are we able to discover the thoughts of the sick and sinning for the purpose of unseeing all that is untrue, and so heal them. Not by mortal mind inquisitiveness, though cloaked with human sincerity, not by digging in the dust bin of material experience, not by prying into forgotten pasts, but simply by growth in spirituality, and the spiritual discernment that is coincident therewith, can we see the errors that may need handling in order to accomplish the healing.

Every one of us is God-endowed with the ability to know the thoughts of those who seek help from us, for the purpose of aiding them. This ability let us daily claim as ours, as an essential faculty of our true selfhood, which cannot be obscured, dulled, or stolen away.

Many a case has been quickly healed, though no habitual error was handled. Other cases may be healed by some uncovering in the patient's thought and his relinquishment of the error without perhaps discussing it with the practitioner. Again, healings often take place when some obstructive error is discerned by the practitioner and reversed by him, but with no apparent need for discussing it with the patient.

The eighty-page chapter on "Christian Science Practice" in *Science and Health* is the longest chapter in this volume. Its frequent and studious perusal will reveal to the individual the correct method of scientific practice as nothing else can do. It shows how best to deal with particular types of sickness and emphasizes that the all-essential need for quick healing is genuine spirituality, expressed in the Mind of Christ.

This never to be lost sight of fact is simply stated by Mrs. Eddy thus: "If the Scientist reaches his patient through divine Love, the healing work will be accomplished at one visit, and the disease will vanish into its native nothingness like dew before the morning sunshine" (*Science and Health*, p. 365).

—*Paul Stark Seeley*

MARY BAKER EDDY: THE ROLE OF LEADER

*T*he discovery of Christian Science by Mary Baker Eddy occupies a definable period in the calendar of history. So does her founding of Christian Science. So does her writing of *Science and Health with Key to the Scriptures* and of the *Manual of The Mother Church*. Without our necessarily pinpointing exact dates, each of these three activities began and has now ended. Each of them continues to bear fresh fruit in human thought and action as we gain new insights into them at ever-deeper levels; but the discovery and founding of Christian Science are now complete, and no changes can be made in Mrs. Eddy's text of *Science and Health* or of the *Church Manual*.

With Mrs. Eddy's leadership of the Christian Science movement it is different. This leadership has no chronological end. It is ongoing and will so remain. On June 3, 1891, the year before Mrs. Eddy reorganized her church as The First Church of Christ, Scientist, a letter from Mrs. Eddy was read at a gathering of her students in Boston. It assured those present: "I am still with you on the field of battle, taking forward marches, broader and higher views, and with the hope that you will follow" (*Miscellaneous Writings*, p. 136). Some two years earlier Mrs. Eddy had moved from Boston to Concord, New Hampshire, and she was to reside in Concord for nearly twenty years; but here she gave notice of her intentions. She had not left the field of her labors or relinquished her leadership.

On Sunday, December 4, 1910, the congregation at morning service in The Mother Church heard an announcement, read from the platform just before the closing benediction. This announcement told of Mrs. Eddy's passing the previous night, and her words quoted above were included in it. From now on The Christian Science Board of Directors, which Mrs. Eddy had established, and the other officers of The Mother Church would bear a new degree of responsibility for discharging the duties Mrs. Eddy had assigned them in the *Church Manual*. But as Leader of the Christian Science movement, Mary Baker Eddy remained and would remain where she had always been, at the head of her followers.

A Leader who follows Christ

At the period Mrs. Eddy first became known as Leader, the terms leader and leadership were generally well regarded. But since World War I certain historical events and social trends have given a somewhat different coloration to these terms. On the one hand leader, leadership, and leader-principle were for some decades closely identified with monstrous political tyrannies. On the other, many individuals and peoples with an increased and wholly proper desire to exercise personal and political self-government have rebelled against strong leadership or what might be regarded as the "star" system in politics and social organization. The combination of these two developments has created in thoughtful circles, certainly throughout democratic nations, a wary suspicion of anyone called a leader or claiming to exercise leadership. Even when a desire for old-fashioned leadership is sometimes expressed, it is more apt to be nostalgic than seriously thought through and meant as a solution for today.

But Christian Scientists are engaged in the Christly mission of redemption, and this includes the redemption of right and useful concepts that may have become soiled by dubious associations. The Discoverer and Founder of Christian Science adopted the title of Leader specifically; in this way she ensured to the Christian Science movement a continuing living leadership. So, while admittedly the terms "leader" and "leadership" have become deeply tainted, this could be one more attempt by animal magnetism to drag down and bury the revelation of the Christ Science and its continuing demonstration on earth. It is up to Christian Scientists in their use of these terms to preserve for them their right and useful significance. For this we need to understand the history and nature of Mrs. Eddy's leadership.

As early as August 1879 the term "Leader," having reference to Mrs. Eddy, began spreading among her followers, and it became increasingly used in the Christian Science periodicals. Finally, as of 1903 Mrs. Eddy gave formal recognition to the term "Leader" in a By-Law in the *Church Manual* (see Art. XXII, Sect. 1).

But in the two years preceding this formal adoption of the term Mrs. Eddy clearly and publicly indicated what the controlling motivation in her leadership would be. Toward the end of her *Message to The Mother Church for 1901*, she concluded a number of instructions to the membership with these words: "obey strictly the laws that be, and follow your Leader only so far as she follows Christ" (p. 34). Then early in her *Message to The Mother Church for 1902*, she reemphasizes the same point: "I again repeat, Follow your Leader, only so far as she follows Christ" (p. 4). The leadership that received formal recognition as of 1903 was not to be arbitrary. It would be under the authority of the Christ, with the Leader of Christian Science humbly following, as she always strove to do, in the steps of the master Christian and Way-shower, Christ Jesus. Mrs. Eddy's leadership is both profoundly scientific and profoundly Christian.

During her life on earth Mrs. Eddy's leadership guided the Christian Science movement as it took its first infant steps and then through its maturing growth and expansion. The story of this period has been recorded in considerable detail by various biographers and by biographical and historical sketches. These show how wisely and resolutely Mrs. Eddy's spiritual perceptions led her Church safely through the many dangers that beset it, whether in the form of open attacks or of more subtle obstruction and resistance.

In those days numerous systems of thought imitated or counterfeited the pure Christ Science she had discovered. In no area was her leadership more needed and more constantly and effectively exercised than in steering the Christian Science movement through this quagmire. Again and again Mrs. Eddy drew the line of separation with wisdom and love but also with unfailing clarity and firmness.

Much can be learned from the study of Mrs. Eddy's leadership during this formative period. But there is also great need that Christian Scientists understand the nature of Mrs. Eddy's continuing leadership right up to the present day and into the future.

Not a personality cult

From early on Mrs. Eddy strenuously opposed any attempt to make her leadership a personality cult, to place her on a pedestal. Her manner toward people was not cold or superior; on the contrary, even during her later years of comparative withdrawal at Concord and Chestnut Hill she expressed warmth, interest, and affection. These qualities in her were apparent to members of her household, to those calling on necessary business or invited to her home, and especially to young children. But constantly by word and deed she encouraged the world to turn away from personality. It was her intent that people

should seek her in her books. There they would most truly find her, as they studied and lived by the potent Christ, Truth, which had been revealed to her. In this way her followers would be led not to person but to Principle, to the divine Truth, for which, as she herself explains, "I was a scribe under orders" (*Mis.*, p. 311).

And so today, as the continuing Leader of Christian Science, Mrs. Eddy does not exercise her leadership through personality or any form of personal presence. Her followers find their guidance in her published writings, which turn them to Christ and to the divine Principle, Love. This leadership, though impersonal, is warm and affectionate. It speaks to each one as to an individual for whom the Leader of Christian Science has a deep love, concern, and interest.

Effective leaders, especially those with a large and dispersed following, have always had to devise methods of ensuring that their communications reach their individual followers without loss of accuracy or impact. Otherwise their message gets lost or distorted as it is passed from mouth to mouth down a chain of command or along from messenger to messenger. But in both the *Church Manual* and in the textbook, *Science and Health*, Mrs. Eddy uniquely solves this problem.

In the *Church Manual* at the head of the list of Church Officers and preceding the By-Laws there stands the name of Rev. Mary Baker Eddy, Pastor Emeritus. Her pastorate emeritus, like her leadership, is thus a continuing office. It ensures individual members of the Christian Science movement that, while loving and supporting those who may from time to time occupy the other church offices and while conscientiously obeying the By-Laws, they will never be separated from the Leader of Christian Science, who is also their Pastor Emeritus.

An incident related by William Dana Orcutt throws light on this point. One day he asked Mrs. Eddy whether he should consult her about certain matters in a way that would require his going over the head of her publisher, Joseph Armstrong. He records that Mrs. Eddy replied, "It will be over no one's head; Mr. Armstrong is engaged to assist me and to carry out my instructions. I am the head" (*Mary Baker Eddy and Her Books* [Boston: The Christian Science Publishing Society, 1950], pp. 58–59). Every church member, turning to the *Church Manual*, has direct access to Mrs. Eddy's continuing impersonal guidance.

Leadership and self-government

In the textbook, as in the *Church Manual*, its author speaks to each individual reader without mediation of time, place, or person. In *Science and Health* she is not addressing herself to a mass readership. She is not addressing her readers from a point in past time or from a localized or any other kind of pedestal, even from the Christian Science Center in Boston. She is addressing them directly in their homes, their offices, their branch churches or Reading Rooms, on land or sea or in the air, anywhere in the world where a single student is reading *Science and Health* or a congregation or small group is hearing it read. And she is addressing each one of them as an individual.

Speaking to each, the Leader of Christian Science says for all times and all places, "I hope, dear reader, I am leading you into the understanding of your divine rights, your heaven-bestowed harmony,—that, as you read, you see there is no cause (outside of erring, mortal, material sense which is not power) able to make you sick or sinful; and I hope that you are conquering this false sense" (*Science and Health*, p. 253).

The leadership of Mrs. Eddy, then, is the leadership of a movement and a church, but it is also a one-to-one leadership. It leads its followers not into subjection—personal, political, or social—but into the understanding of individual divine rights and into freedom from every kind of enslavement. "God has endowed man," writes Mrs. Eddy, "with inalienable rights, among which are self-government, reason, and conscience. Man is properly self-governed only when he is guided rightly and governed by his Maker, divine Truth and Love" (p. 106). True leadership bears no relationship to the tyrannous political systems of this century nor to anything that would lessen individual self-reliance. The end product of true leadership, as exemplified in Mrs. Eddy's leadership and in her following of the Christ, is universal spiritual self-government fulfilling the creative purpose of divine Truth and Love. Its discipline is the strictest yet most flexible of all disciplines, self-discipline; and it makes no one surrender a newly found and newly liberated identity.

The future of leadership

What of the future? A figure of speech borrowed by Mrs. Eddy from the parables of Jesus is that of the leaven. She expected the teachings of Christian Science to leaven, to penetrate and transform the scientific, religious, and medical thinking of her day and indeed the thinking behind every human activity. And this is already happening, though often unrecognized even by Christian Scientists. The identifiable Christian Science movement, with its edifices, activities, and membership, is only a small part of the progress Mrs. Eddy's leadership of Christian Science has brought to an awakening world.

As the effect of the leaven increases, it is likely that there may appear more and more approximations to the Science of Christ. These, while progressive and praiseworthy, may not recognize their debt to the Christ Science and in thought and conduct, or in both, may fall short of its purity. Then just as Mrs. Eddy's leadership brought the early Christian Scientists through the imitations and counterfeits, as explained already, so her leadership will bring Christian Scientists of today and tomorrow safely through any temptation to be satisfied with the approximations. She will continue to lead her movement forward with the pure Word of Truth while the approximations are being further leavened and brought to the point of their final yielding to the fullness of Christian Science and its demonstration.

Inasmuch as Mrs. Eddy follows Christ, her leadership is part of the unfolding mission of salvation—to save, not to condemn, the world that God so loved and so loves. This mission goes back through the pages of the Bible to the beginnings of human history. It must reach forward through history until the human story yields finally to the divine fact—man revealed in God's likeness, wholly spiritual and complete.

The Psalmist prayed to God, "O send out thy light and thy truth: let them lead me'" (Ps. 43:3). This was the spirit of Christ Jesus' prayer as exemplified in his whole life. This was the spirit of Mrs. Eddy's prayer as she followed the Christ. And this is the prayer of all Christian Scientists as they follow their Leader in the footsteps of Christ, Truth.

—*Peter J. Henniker-Heaton*

MIND SEES

Sight is an eternal faculty of infinite Mind, God. It is not organic and transient. Man, being God's idea, is endowed with this discernment—clear, distinct, and permanent.

Sight is the all-seeing activity of divine consciousness. This faculty is included in the omni-action of God. Its range is infinite, expressing the omnipresence of Mind; its clarity reflects the brilliance of Truth; its focus manifests the unchanging precision of divine Principle; and its permanency rests on the eternality of the one Ego. Thus true sight manifests the range, clarity, focus, and eternality of the divine consciousness.

Immortal Mind is the one self-existent cause, expressing itself in man and the universe. Mind's ideas are held within divine consciousness; they can never be external to it. The nature of every idea, its substance and form, is conceived and maintained by Mind. The creator is eternally conscious of every idea, both in its outline and in every delicate detail of its identity.

Man is the highest idea of Mind. His discernment is not a separate faculty but is a manifestation of the all-seeing Mind. Man clearly perceives his source, his own identity, and his relation to his Maker.

Mind being infinite, there is no opposing power to mar true vision, no separation between Mind and its image. There can be no mist in the infinitude of Truth. The faculty of sight cannot deteriorate or be destroyed. It remains forever intact.

Mortal sense contradicts these facts. It depicts man as physically sensate, insisting that sight is a fleshly faculty, organic and temporal.

This mist, the material sense of existence, is the basic error underlying sight problems. The Christ pierces this mist with the light of Truth. In *Science and Health* Mrs. Eddy writes, "Science declares that Mind, not matter, sees, hears, feels, speaks" (p. 485).

The prophet foresaw the power of the Christ "to open the blind eyes, to bring out the prisoners from the prison, and them that sit in darkness out of the prison house" (Isa. 42:7). Christ Jesus' healing ministry fulfilled this prophecy of Isaiah. When Jesus healed the congenitally blind man he declared: "Neither hath this man sinned, nor his parents: but that the works of God should be made manifest in him" and "For judgment I am come into this world, that they which see not might see" (John 9:3, 39).

The same curative power of Christ can be demonstrated in the twentieth century. Through individual acceptance of the revelation of Christian Science, the light of Truth melts the fog of material sense and heals deficient physical sight. This sacred office of the Christ reveals the works of God: incorporeal man and his God-given ability to perceive God's creation.

A sight difficulty can be overcome with the specific truth that destroys the specific error. Fear can be dissolved by the realization that the source of man's perception is unfailing Love, for Mind and Love are one. The belief in diseased eyes can be refuted with affirmations of the unchanging perfection of being. Such difficulties are mortal mind's negations of reality. They can never affect the real faculty of sight.

The Christian Science healer turns away from material factors—from optical focus, physical light, and the viewing of matter. Healing comes through dematerialization of thought and the clear discernment of spiritual reality. It demonstrates the scientific fact that Mind—not matter—sees.

The fundamental truths of genuine sight are the infinity of Mind and the eternal oneness of Mind and its ideas. Whatever would separate thought from the spiritual ideal needs to be recognized as a false imposition and denied reality. All false evidence must be detected and negated. This correction brings human consciousness into closer unity with divine Mind, and to the dawning of reality, the demonstration of true vision.

As human thought grasps the facts of existence, it will cease to be beclouded by vague material theories. The faltering steps of blind belief in Truth will be exchanged for enlightened faith and inspired conviction.

The opacity of selfishness needs to be dissolved through a clearer apprehension of universal divine Love. The restricted view of self-centered thought needs to be replaced with the limitless perspective of unselfed love. The darkness of self-righteousness must yield before a humble recognition of the one

Ego. The gross blindness of sensuality needs to be replaced by the light of pure spirituality. Human thought must become a clearer transparency for divine Truth and Love.

The belief in aging and its effects on human sight needs to be firmly denied. Human birth, development, and decline are not the true record of man. Because sight is not dependent upon physical structure, it is not subject to deterioration. Such false beliefs can be rejected. One need not let his activities become increasingly restricted. Instead, he can gain expanding views of reality, nullifying any beliefs of failing sight. Man is the expression of the unchanging Ego. He manifests the eternal newness and vigor of Life, the permanency of divine Being.

Heredity is a belief of mortal mind that needs to be strongly refuted. Man is not a mortal under a curse. As God's idea, he is eternally blessed, is not a mortal at all. The supposed law of heredity is a counterfeit of God's law and can be proved unreal. Freedom from so-called hereditary sight defects is gained by the denial of a mortal origin and the recognition of man's source as the one divine Parent, who endows His offspring with His own perfect faculties.

Accident has no place in the divine order. Perceptivity is not in transitory matter. It is in and of Spirit. Therefore it is indestructible. Man's discernment is maintained by the one eternal cause. Understanding the permanency of sight, one can demonstrate it.

Distressing memories should not be allowed to darken human consciousness. They can be erased by the realization that the real man knows only the unchanging harmony of being. And fear of the future can be replaced with the recognition that good is ever unfolding. When thought is magnifying God, it cannot at the same time be apprehensive and gloomy.

The one divine consciousness clearly perceives both the vastness and the infinitesimals of infinite creation. Only mortal mind regards objects as material and external to consciousness, and imposes limitations of nearsightedness and farsightedness on itself.

In reality, color is a quality of Soul and includes beauty and radiance. It is an aspect of character and identity. Man is spiritually sensitive, never blinded to the infinite variety of color in God's creation.

And the human being's realization of these truths can overcome the belief of colorblindness.

There is no inherent or developed weakness in any element of real being, including sight. Every identity expresses the unfailing strength of Spirit. No strain or exhaustion can exist in Mind's faculties. Genuine discernment can know no fatigue and no overaction. These truths outshine belief in weak eyesight.

Mrs. Eddy states, "When a so-called material sense is lost, and Truth restores that lost sense,—on the basis that all consciousness is Mind and eternal, —the former position, that sense is organic and material, is proven erroneous" (*No and Yes*, p. 10).

In his *Historical Sketches* Clifford P. Smith wrote: "In November, 1884, when Mrs. Eddy lived in Boston, a lady called on her and said, 'I am blind… .' In her reply, Mrs. Eddy spoke of goodness and health as more natural than badness and disease. She also spoke of one's duty to praise God and of one's need to leave evidences material for evidences spiritual. The lady said, 'I can see a little better,' and went her way. Within a week she sent a message to Mrs. Eddy saying that her sight was perfectly restored" (*Historical Sketches* [Boston: The Christian Science Publishing Society, 1941], pp. 71–72).

With diligence and humility we need to exercise the divine faculty of sight. As our thought becomes spiritualized, we will discern spiritual reality more and more distinctly. We will demonstrate true sight in all its clarity, focus, and permanence. We will prove that not matter but divine Mind sees!

—*Hazel Willoughby Harrison*

NOTHING TO FEAR

Have you ever gone to a masquerade party? Everyone goes as someone he or she is not. The masquerader assumes a different identity and takes great pleasure in confusing people. With his identity masked, the masquerader is emboldened to do things he would never attempt if his true identity were discerned.

The chief masquerader of all time is the false, lying conception variously named in the Bible *Satan, Lucifer, devil, serpent, dragon, carnal mind, liar, evil spirit.* Isaiah quotes Lucifer as saying: "I will ascend above the heights of the clouds; I will be like the most High." (Isa. 14:14) What a presumptuous masquerader—evil masquerading as good! And we're often taken in by this phase of evil. In fact, there's even a name for people who present an innocent front, while behind the "mask" they're quietly preparing to attack: wolves in sheep's clothing. Such was Judas Iscariot, Christ Jesus' unfaithful disciple. Judas sat with his Master at their last supper, his benign appearance masking a deceitful plot. But Jesus' pure spiritual consciousness was undeceived by evil. He was able to see through the mask and foretell exactly what Judas was going to do.

Mary Baker Eddy, who discovered and founded Christian Science, referred to this lying presumption—the discordant action of mortal mind—in such terms as *animal magnetism, mesmerism, hypnotism, occultism, necromancy,* and *malpractice.* She removed its mask and mystery as she further defined it as "aggressive mental suggestion" (*Manual of The Mother Church,* p. 42). The evil is aggressive because it pushes, assaults, and attacks. It's mental because the aggression takes place within thought. And it's suggestion because it's something that's *put into* thought.

Animal magnetism substitutes bad for good, and wrong for right. It sows confusion and dissension. It makes danger look safe, and safety look dangerous. It turns things upside down and makes them appear to be right side up. It's hypnotic because it makes things seem to be what they're not. And it engenders fear because there's no safety or stability in the supposed absence of God, infinite Love, the divine Principle of all good.

In fact, fear is a major channel through which animal magnetism attempts to work. Fear presents evil as real, and is therefore a basic element of animal magnetism. It proudly carries on its banner the little word, "if." "*If* this happens. *If* this doesn't stop. *If* this turns out to be serious." This suggestion, in turn, engenders doubt. And underlying all fear is the belief that there is something to fear because God, total good, is not All. But God says, "I am Love, and I am All. In Me, in divine Love, there is nothing to fear, because in My allness, there is nothing unlike Myself. In Me, there *is* no fear."

Divine Love is infinite good, total good. And this totality of good is the antidote for fear, because just as light and darkness can't exist together, Love and fear can't exist together. And just as darkness doesn't *battle* light but is *dispelled* by light; so fear doesn't battle Love, but is dispelled by Love. When viewed from the vantage point of divine Love, animal magnetism with its fear is seen as the unreal essence of a suppositional, unreal mortal mind. And that's the acme of *nothing!* The only way animal magnetism can claim reality is to make us believe in it or fear it.

The entire claim of animal magnetism is an illusion, a belief of mind in matter, a belief in a power and presence apart from God. And because there can *be* no power or presence apart from omnipotent, omnipresent God, the illusion is unreal and powerless. But its apparent masquerading ability makes it a lie that must be regularly detected and unmasked, lest it pass itself off as a power and presence apart from, coequal with, or superior to, God.

The Christ, the manifestation of divine Love that animated Jesus' life, is the voice of Truth that constantly unmasks error because it's always speaking to human consciousness. It's constantly telling us what is real about ourselves. And what is that reality? That we are right now the sons and daughters of God. Right now we are the image of God, Spirit, and are safe and loved in divine Love's care. But the voiceless voice of false suggestion sometimes whispers to our thought to try to make us believe what is not true or real about us. If we would detect the whisper of evil—often expressed as fear—as not being part of our thought but as an imposition *on* our thought, we wouldn't fear fear!

This became quite evident to me some years back when I found myself going through a period of severe pain, unable to carry on my regular activities. It grew worse over several months and those subtle "What if" suggestions began to knock on my mental door.

Then I began to see the hypnotic nature of the fear and how it was trying to talk to me. I knew that fear was no part of divine Mind, God. And I knew that I expressed that Mind, so the fear couldn't be something that originated in me. It had to be something that was being imposed on my thought. Darkness couldn't invade light, and fear and doubt couldn't invade the confidence and assurance inspired by my knowledge that God is Love. I read this statement by Mrs. Eddy: "Forget not for a moment, that God is All-in-all—therefore, that in reality there is but one cause and effect" (*Miscellaneous Writings 1883-1896*, pp. 154–155).

That was the challenge to me. Could I be made to forget the spiritual facts that I knew to be true? What were some of those facts? That God, the one divine Mind, is All. That Mind knows itself and its own allness. That there is no outside to that knowing. That pain with its fear, and fear with its pain, are no part of divine Mind. That they're outside of ever-presence, and so must have no presence. And that they're the supposed phenomenon of nothing, having no law, authority, or lasting power.

Hypnotic fear had riveted my thought to that false image of a power that wasn't and to a presence that wasn't. I found I could say with full assurance to the condition facing me, "Even though I think I feel you, I know you're not there. Even though I think I see you, I know you're not there. What God knows about me as His own likeness is true right now."

Jesus showed the link between what we understand and what we experience in our body when he said, "The light of the body is the eye: if therefore thine eye be single, thy whole body shall be full of light" (Matt. 6:22). And Hebrews expresses it this way: "The word of God is quick, and powerful, and sharper than any two-edged sword, piercing even to the dividing asunder of soul and spirit, and of the joints and marrow, and is a discerner of the thoughts and intents of the heart" (Heb. 4:12).

The more I considered and understood God—His allness, and His onlyness—the more I felt His great love for me. That love of God who is divine Love itself contains no fear, no pain, nothing to cause inflammation or infection. The torment of pain and the torment of fear that had appeared together, disappeared together. Fear lost its grip on me and the pain left.

What did this prove? That the masquerader had been completely unmasked. I recognized my true, unchanging spiritual identity as the forever fact of my being—and it's the fact of everyone's being. We are not of the flesh. We're the sons and daughters of God, divine Love. And in that Love we're guarded, guided, and cherished. That's the Love that not only unmasks animal magnetism but also casts out fear and its effects.

—*James Spencer*

ON WHICH SIDE
ARE YOU ARGUING?

ᴁvery student of Christian Science knows that its teachings give one a new way of thinking, a new outlook, a new standpoint for thought and action.

One finds marvelous inspiration and joy in learning the absolute truths of God's omnipotent goodness and man's true being as God's spiritual idea. He naturally loves the grand truths of being and draws on them for strength, comfort, peace—which they certainly bring in buoyant and abundant measure.

Yet we soon find we cannot merely bask in a euphoric bliss of accepting these truths as theory. They have to be *lived*—made practical moment by moment. We come to realize that our thoughts and conclusions must be tested by the standard of Science, the standard of Truth. In other words, we see the necessity of really facing our own thoughts. We see how important it is to challenge the thoughts that knock at our mental door, and to accept only those that are valid and worthy in the light of Science.

Numerous times in her writings our Leader, Mary Baker Eddy, stresses how vital this sifting of thoughts is in metaphysical healing. For example, she writes: "The sick unconsciously argue for suffering, instead of against it. They admit its reality, whereas they should deny it. They should plead in opposition to the testimony of the deceitful senses, and maintain man's immortality and eternal likeness to God" (*Science and Health with Key to the Scriptures*, pp. 394–395).

She shows us clearly that to argue on behalf of symptoms or appearances of disease would limit our ability to demonstrate Mind's power to heal; that it would amount to arguing against our own success in healing. As she tells us, "Your influence for good depends upon the weight you throw into the right scale" (*Science and Health*, p. 192).

In fact, Christian Science broadens the application of the ninth commandment, "Thou shalt not bear false witness against thy neighbour" (Ex. 20:16), to provide a standard of spiritually scientific truth and honesty for all our thoughts. Mrs. Eddy writes: "'Thou shalt not bear false witness;' that is, thou shalt not utter a lie, either mentally or audibly, nor cause it to be thought." Then, referring to several of the Commandments, including this one, she adds, "Obedience to these commandments is indispensable to health, happiness, and length of days" (*Miscellaneous Writings*, p. 67).

To heal in Christian Science we need to contend vigorously for the truths of God's omnipotence and man's spiritual integrity, and to deny the supposed reality of sickness as well as sin. This method of fervent prayer—acknowledging unreservedly the power and allness of God as infinite Mind, Love, and Life—opens the way for the energies of Spirit to restore the sufferer, and for a palpable sense of Love's sustaining presence to melt away pain and terror.

On the other hand, arguing (even with good intentions) on behalf of the supposed validity and activity of disease, sin, or death in their myriad forms constitutes destructive malpractice. It violates the commandment, "Thou shalt not bear false witness."

The point made here applies to the health of our national and international society as well as to that of individuals. Widely publicized predictions of disease, disaster, and chaos are a kind of unwitting malpractice—particularly in the dramatic and incessant forms so prevalent today in the media. If unresisted, these tend to be self-fulfilling; at very least they are a fear-producing, depressive influence tending to paralyze constructive remedial thought. The prevalence of this miasmic atmosphere prompts one to be grateful for *The Christian Science Monitor*, which succeeds to a remarkable degree in reporting public events realistically without indulging in negative predictions. It is cause for gratitude also for the Science that shows us how to deal with destructive thoughts through prayer.

The point applies to church activity too. If we feel dissatisfied with decisions made or the way we perceive things to be done, do we argue (more or less unconsciously) on behalf of the reality of ineptitude, lack of wisdom, or dismal prospects? Or do we earnestly pray to understand that there is only one omnipotent Mind and that this Mind alone governs all things—including "the kingdom of men" (v. 25) as brought out in the fourth chapter of Daniel? If we feel that those around us are not adhering to the standard of Science, do we spend our time in criticizing, or in spiritual knowing?

From the time the Church of Christ, Scientist, was established, its detractors have been systematically predicting its downfall. Are we going to join the predictors and become witnesses on behalf of vigorously pushed aggressive mental suggestions of failure?

Sometimes a sincere worker will ask: "What can we do in a situation where an influential member exerts a divisive influence that's splitting the congregation?" Even here, isn't the basic conviction of all Christian Scientists still valid, namely, that spiritually scientific, silent prayer is the most effective means of unmasking and neutralizing the wiles of animal magnetism, settling human discords, and assuring progress and healing?

Unquestionably it takes a great deal of moral and spiritual courage to argue truthfully on behalf of the spiritual facts of being when all the evidence of "the deceitful senses" pulls in the opposite direction. But our God is a living God—irresistibly outpouring Love—whose healing influence and surging powers of attraction profoundly change the standpoint of human thinking. Mrs. Eddy helps us demonstrate this when she writes: "The way to extract error from mortal mind is to pour in truth through flood-tides of Love" (*Science and Health*, p. 201). The more we let those "flood-tides" prevail in our individual consciousness, the more effectively we will be able to bring healing to ourselves and others.

—*DeWitt John*

THE PILATE ASSUMPTION

The moment must have been tense, even dramatic. Christ Jesus didn't respond to his interrogator. Pilate pressed him: "Speakest thou not unto me? knowest thou not that I have power to crucify thee, and have power to release thee?" With unshaken confidence Jesus answered, "Thou couldest have no power at all against me, except it were given thee from above" (John 19:10, 11).

One can hardly read of such episodes leading to the crucifixion without being deeply touched. Pilate's assumption that he could determine Jesus' fate; Jesus' certainty that God alone was controlling his destiny: these two views have implications way beyond that significant event when those two men faced each other.

The Pilate assumption challenges us even today. And it threatened people long before Jesus' time. What Pilate said symbolized a basic mortal fallacy: the belief that people, places, events, can exercise final control over our lives. Moses, in preparing to lead the Israelites out of Egypt, must have felt the arrogance of the Pilate assumption in the confrontation with Pharaoh; Elijah felt it with Jezebel; the three young Hebrews with King Nebuchadnezzar and his fiery furnace.

And what about events in your own life? Is there a Pilate speaking to you, warning of its control over your destiny? Perhaps a medical verdict? Unemployment statistics? A domineering acquaintance? If so, surrender to the Christ just as Jesus did. Accepting our native Christliness, we will find the conviction welling up in us, "Thou couldest have no power at all against me, except it were given thee from above."

This is a different kind of prayer from one in which we attempt to brush away the Pilate confronting us—or justify ourselves before him. Perhaps Jesus could have answered Pilate so convincingly that the governor would simply have released him. The resurrection would have been lost to the world. Some of our own challenges (modest in comparison) may impel a pleading to change the events; yet they may call more for a deep recognition that nothing in the development of our career is beyond God's authority.

Does this mean that we simply must accept whatever happens as God's will—suffering, limitation, inharmony? Surely not. It means rather that we so thoroughly deepen our conviction of God's reign in our affairs that all actions are drawn into conformity with His plan. Our destiny is never determined by other people, by places or events, when we surrender to the purpose divine Mind has designed for us. Of this omniscient Mind that is God, Mrs. Eddy writes, "He has mercy upon us, and guides every event of our careers" (*Unity of Good*, pp. 3–4).

Let's take an example. Suppose a foreman on the job is obstructing our progress. Maybe he or she has been unfair, heavy-handed, even antagonistic. Perhaps we have prayed earnestly to be moved to another position—or better yet that the obnoxious foreman be moved! And still no solution. Could it be that in this case our answer just isn't in that kind of prayer? In Science we do not pray for humanly outlined solutions; we pray to know divine Mind's all power and intelligent government of man. Think of what it would mean to approach this challenge more from the standpoint, "Thou couldest have no power at all against me, except it were given thee from above."

Such a perspective may seem at first almost untenable. "How could this person, who is doing something so wrong, be impelled by God?" you wonder. But that's not the point. Jesus wasn't marveling over some sort of spiritually inspired action on Pilate's part. He was challenging the assumption that *anyone* could stand in the way of his divinely impelled purpose. Jesus had an overriding conviction that nothing, absolutely nothing, could block the path that God was mapping out for him. And on that basis he saw that even those who thought they were thwarting his purpose could only contribute to his full demonstration of immortal Life.

Today the Pilate assumption would try to operate in a variety of ways. Our response is crucial. Most people accept the assumption. Then try to battle this supposed authority. Yet the Christly approach is to reject the assumption in the first place; and know God's omnipotence, His unimpaired command, with such conviction and clarity that the actions and attitudes of others actually push us forward rather than defeat or frustrate us.

The only way we can truly challenge the Pilate assumption, effectively and permanently, is through a discernment of where we are really going. If we are just wandering along through human experience, there will be plenty of times when various Pilates will claim power to crucify or release us.

But if we realize we're moving directly and specifically toward an understanding that man is God's perfect idea, unflawed by mortality, then we won't be held in the grip of a false assumption. Jesus knew where he was going. Pilate didn't stop him. The crucifixion didn't stop him. He perceived that all those events were speeding his resurrection— his emergence from the belief of substance and life in matter. Because Jesus saw God's controlling hand in every aspect of his life, the ascension itself awaited him.

We too can recognize God's presence leading our lives. And whatever would oppose our progress will be overturned; it will become a support. We will experience more of the resurrection; and eventually our ascension.

—Nathan A. Talbot

"PRACTICAL, OPERATIVE CHRISTIAN SCIENCE"

To her students Mary Baker Eddy, the beloved Discoverer and Founder of Christian Science, extends an invitation. She says (*Miscellaneous Writings*, pp. 206–207): "As you journey, and betimes sigh for rest 'beside the still waters,' ponder this lesson of love. Learn its purpose; and in hope and faith, where heart meets heart reciprocally blest, drink with me the living waters of the spirit of my life-purpose,—to impress humanity with the genuine recognition of practical, operative Christian Science." The waters we are to drink are not stale and stagnant, but living waters, sparkling and fresh from the depths of infinity; nor are we invited to drink them alone, but with her, for she says, "drink with me." As we share the spirit of her life purpose, namely "to impress humanity with the genuine recognition of practical, operative Christian Science," we may feel the presence of her great love, even the divine Love which reflects itself in her love for all mankind.

Mrs. Eddy knew that in order to understand and accept Christian Science, the world had to understand and accept her. And today humanity's great need is to gain a clearer, higher concept of her. To acknowledge the revelator is to acknowledge the revelation; to disbelieve the revelator is to disbelieve the revelation. Jesus knew the importance of a true evaluation of Truth's mouthpiece. In his discourse with his disciples, as recorded in the sixteenth chapter of Matthew, he rejected what the world said about him and opened their eyes to look above the person to the divinity of his being. And so in evaluating our Leader, we must look above the person to the divinity of the Science she revealed. Mrs. Eddy cannot be separated from the Science she discovered. We cannot understand the Science without understanding her; nor can we understand her without proportionately gaining a clearer understanding of the Science.

Mrs. Eddy refers to the trials and sufferings which led to her great discovery as God's gracious preparation. She translates all her trials back into love, and yet from the human standpoint her experience was one of heartbreak and hardship. In our seemingly bitter experiences can we not see only the preparation of divine Love for higher, holier work? We must understand that this Science is the final revelation and that her book *Science and Health with Key to the Scriptures* is its complete and forever textbook.

What was it that was revealed to Mrs. Eddy as the secret of the Master's healing ministry? What was it that she discovered? It was something that Jesus proved but that the world had not seen—not even its deepest thinkers—and something which stirred the carnal mind to its depths, namely the nothingness of matter.

She understood what Jesus meant when he defined God as Spirit (see John 4:24). And she saw that Spirit is omnipotence, the only power everywhere; omnipresence, the only presence; and omniscience, the only Truth, or true knowledge; and these facts necessarily meant the nothingness—the nonexistence—of matter.

She discovered that God is Mind and that therefore all that exists must exist in Mind as a manifestation of Mind; and thus she reduced matter to a false belief, and supposititious manifestation of a supposititious mind, an illusion. She saw that if you take away this false mind, you take away matter, for without a mind to form it and cognize it matter would have neither form, substance, life, nor intelligence; in other words, it would not exist. It is essential that we see this point, for it is basic to the practice of Christian Science.

There are no contradictions, no inconsistencies, in our Leader's writings. In exquisite beauty of language and from the heights of pure inspiration she shows us the things of Spirit, and with the penetrating searchlight of Truth she exposes the nothingness of matter. And she shows us how to prove this. Had Mrs. Eddy ignored the claims of evil, the revelation would not have been correctly stated. It would not have withstood the onslaughts of mortal mind. So long as there remains in belief a claim of evil, just so long must Truth stand as its denial.

Christian Science rests on one Principle, and from this Principle emanates one law. Both the Principle and its operation are infallible. There are no offshoots of Christian Science, no improvements upon it. Adulterations of it are meaningless.

The clarion call of "practical, operative Christian Science" is (Matt. 10:8), "Heal the sick, cleanse the lepers, raise the dead, cast out devils," or demons.

It is a call to action. So important did our Leader consider this call that she makes it, together with the cross and crown, the official seal on all her published writings.

Our Leader's discovery was not an intellectual theory. It was not the product of human reason. It was pure revelation, the result of her diligent search for Truth. She was healed; and the healing told her she had discovered the spiritual law for which she searched. But she had to go further. As she pursued the quest, reason and revelation coincided and led her to divine heights. Every Christian Scientist has to follow in her footsteps, and in a certain sense each has to discover the healing Principle for himself. Intellectual proficiency in the letter of Christian Science is not enough. It is the spirit that heals, and Mrs. Eddy warns us that the spirit reaches humanity only in small degrees. We must work for it, pray for it, cherish it, and *live* it.

Mrs. Eddy expects every one of her followers to heal. The early Christians were healers. The strength of our movement is its healing activity. In the *Manual of The Mother Church*, under the caption "Healing Better than Teaching" (Art. XXX, Sect. 7), our Leader refers to the practice of each member of this Church. None is excluded. There must be radical self-purification, deep, soul-searching sincerity, and daily demonstration.

With the Master the thing that characterized his ministry, that identified him as the Messiah, was healing—that was the proof that what he said was truth; healing was the very substance of his ministry. The multitudes flocked to him because of the love he radiated. Of the Christ, Truth, which he demonstrated, Mrs. Eddy says (*Miscellaneous Writings*, p. 200), "The master Metaphysician understood omnipotence to be All-power: because Spirit was to him All-in-all, matter was palpably an error of premise and conclusion, while God was the only substance, Life, and intelligence of man."

To those who would follow him, Jesus said, "Ye must be born again" (John 3:7). Of himself he said, "The prince of this world cometh, and hath nothing in me" (John 14:30). He did nothing of himself; he knew it was the Father who did the works. He gave error no response; he was never afraid of it, never mesmerized by it, never appalled by its enormity, never dismayed by its seeming tenacity. He was sure of his dominion because he was sure of his oneness with God. The spirituality of his thinking was his protection and his power.

This spirituality was the Christ. It enabled him to discern with scientific accuracy the error he would destroy and to replace it with the spiritual fact, the evidence that nothing was present but God and His idea. He demonstrated the practicality and Science of the Christianity he taught.

Our loved Leader was the outstanding healer of this age. Her revelation was ushered in with spiritual healing. As a result of her lifework, the Protestant churches are looking into Christian healing as they never have before. True, they are largely trying to heal spiritually on a material basis, trying to mix drugs with the power of Spirit, a basis from which it cannot be done; but they are feeling the urge that Christianity must heal.

Our Leader's writings are full of the records of her healing work; so are her authentic biographies. It was as natural for Mrs. Eddy to heal as for the sun to shine. Like Jesus, she was never mesmerized by the material senses. She demonstrated the power, the presence, the allness of Spirit. Her revelation uncovered the workings of animal magnetism. Up to that time, they had been hidden. She discovered the subtlety of evil and proved the nothingness of it. She taught her followers how to pray.

Christian Science shows us the need of facing and challenging with Truth not only the obvious faults in oneself but the latent beliefs of sensuality, fear, lust—all those subtle, latent errors that mortal mind claims lie dormant, unseen, and almost unknown in one's mentality. It is the latent belief that life is in matter that has to be overcome in each of us. The searchlight of Truth must be turned within, not in morbid introspection, but with the penetration of Soul that Love may engrave upon the understanding and heart its own precious image. The daily metaphysical work each student must do for himself must include a deep and earnest prayer for self-purification.

In the measure that we understand Christian Science there will be no desire for material methods of healing, no divided allegiance between matter and Spirit. Christian Science can take no secondary place in our lives. First, last, and always we are Christian Scientists. Christ, Truth, must be supreme in our affections, supreme in our lives.

If we would drink with our loved Leader "the living waters of the spirit" of her life purpose, our concept of church must grow and grow. We must come to understand the divine meaning and spiritual idea of Church, even the Church Universal and Triumphant, which springs from the heart of divinity. We must see the Church she founded as the human exponent of this ideal. Thus we may claim for our Church the Master's benediction when he said (Matt. 16:18), "Upon this rock [Peter's recognition of the Christ] I will build my church; and the gates of hell shall not prevail against it." His words are infallible; his promise is perpetual.

The Mother Church and its branches represent Mrs. Eddy's work as Founder. She founded her Church upon the rock of Truth. Her prayer for her followers was that they might find within it home and heaven. Let us bring out the heaven in our church work. Then we shall find home, an abiding sense of Love's gracious outpouring of comfort, security, and rest.

Our Leader foresaw the dangers threatening society, and she saw the role of the Church of Christ, Scientist. She saw too the demand Church makes upon each member, the demand of loyalty and obedience. To this end she gave us *The Mother Church Manual*, with its Rules and By-Laws, its tender guidance and priceless admonitions. The Section "Guidance of Members" is one each member should heed daily. St. Paul defines "church" in his first letter to Timothy as "the pillar and ground of the truth" (3:15). The Church of Christ, Scientist, has a tremendous mission, because the Science of Christianity must become the universal religion and therapeutics.

Mrs. Eddy writes in *The First Church of Christ, Scientist, and Miscellany* (p. 125), "The hour is come; the bride (Word) is adorned, and lo, the bridegroom cometh!" And then she asks the pertinent question, "Are our lamps trimmed and burning?"

To accept our Leader's invitation and drink with her "the living waters of the spirit" of her life purpose presents a formidable challenge. But behold its reward—humanity blessed, its affections enriched, by the demonstration of "practical, operative Christian Science."

—*L. Ivimy Gwalter*

THE PRAYER THAT "COVERS ALL HUMAN NEEDS"

Chere are very few Christians who are not familiar with the words of the brief prayer that Christ Jesus gave to his disciples when he taught them how to pray. In fact this prayer, just a simple eight lines in many Bibles, is repeated by millions of people, millions of times daily throughout the world.

When we pray this prayer, do we really expect *all* our needs to be met, and to be healed as a result of praying it? If we expect results from prayer, why does this prayer not bring instantaneous results every time it is uttered? Is there a missing ingredient somewhere?

In her book *Science and Health with Key to the Scriptures*, Christian Science Founder Mary Baker Eddy concluded the first chapter, entitled "Prayer," with her spiritual interpretation of this all-encompassing prayer, which she said "covers all human needs" (see pp. 16–17). But perhaps the missing ingredient for instantaneous and certain healing is to be found in these words, "Only as we rise above all material sensuousness and sin, can we reach the heaven-born aspiration and spiritual consciousness, which is indicated in the Lord's Prayer and which instantaneously heals the sick" (p. 16).

So this is the prayer of "heaven-born aspiration and spiritual consciousness." It is the prayer of spiritual sense that rises above "material sensuousness and sin." It is not a prayer of the head, but of the heart. It is of God, not of man. It is selfless and soaring, and breathes the inspiration of God's allness.

This prayer is one of continuous affirmation of God's presence and power, and of our oneness with our divine Father-Mother. It reveals God's all-harmonious nature, and the exact same nature for man. It explains that God's kingdom of harmony has already come and is ever present. Also that His incontestable loving will is supreme, and is being done now and always, here and everywhere.

The Lord's Prayer affirms that because of the tender family relationship between man and God, humanity is always and continuously supplied with grace to meet every circumstance, love to meet every difficult human relationship, and total immunity from sickness, sin, and death. It rejoices that the only place is His heavenly kingdom, the only power is His unopposable presence, and that His light and glory are infinite, eternal, and the only reality there is. What an affirmation and statement of perfection!

Every time we pray this prayer we can gain fresh inspiration and become more aware of the recurring theme song that the words imply. This is indeed the "heaven-born aspiration and spiritual consciousness" that is its essential ingredient and is available to all.

Our Father which art in heaven
Our Father-Mother God, all-harmonious

Jesus said, "Call no man your father upon the earth: for one is your Father, which is in heaven" (Matt. 23:9), and this is echoed in Mrs. Eddy's words: "Jesus acknowledged no ties of the flesh. . . . He recognized Spirit, God, as the only creator, and therefore as the Father of all" (*Science and Health*, p. 31). These truths free us from all the restrictions of material living, its hereditary beliefs, limitations, and mortal genetics. The tender, loving relationship with our one Father-Mother, God, endows us with our true inheritance, and all the glorious qualities of both manhood and womanhood; the tenderness, beauty, and love of Motherhood; and the strength, understanding, and vigor of Fatherhood. It reveals who we really are.

Hallowed be Thy name
Adorable One

God and man are one. There is only one Life, one Mind, one Being, and it is God revealing Himself as our unoptional perfection. The Adorable One, which is God and man, includes nothing discordant or inharmonious, and thus our nature, like God's, is always adorable, the same as God.

Thy kingdom come
Thy kingdom is come; Thou art ever-present

God's kingdom, His reign of harmony, peace, and well-being, is not something that is on the horizon or on the way; it is already here and now, in spite of what the material senses may say. This is the prayer of the acknowledgment of present good, now. This kingdom is *within* us, as Jesus said, and it is a kingdom of all good. Mary Baker Eddy wrote: "What is the kingdom of heaven? The abode of Spirit, the realm of the real.

No matter is there, no night is there—nothing that maketh or worketh a lie. Is this kingdom afar off? No: it is ever-present here" (*Miscellaneous Writings 1883-1896*, p. 174).

Perfection is not delayed or postponed. Right now, all being is God expressing Himself, and all we have to do is to joyously acknowledge this ever-present realm of divine well-being and abundance. It *is here*, right now!

Thy will be done in earth, as it is in heaven

Enable us to know,—as in heaven, so on earth,—God is omnipotent, supreme

God's will is the activity of divine Love, blessing all and allowing nothing but good to be manifested in His creation. His will is final, incontestable, irrevocable. No schemes of a counterfeit mind can usurp the place and power of God's ever-present will. Human outlining is not the divine will in action, and a true willingness to let divine Mind express itself as our Life will lift us out of doubt, uncertainty, or fear of present or future events. The will of God is always good and is always right, and His will alone is being done.

Give us this day our daily bread

Give us grace for to-day; feed the famished affections

When we affirm the absolute certainty of good, it naturally follows that man, as God's loved child, is always supplied with what he needs. He is given daily bread, which, according to Mrs. Eddy, embraces grace, obedience, and love (*Miscellaneous Writings*, p. 127). One dictionary defines *grace* as "the divine influence ever-operative in man to regenerate and sanctify." The Bible says that Jesus was "filled with wisdom: and the grace of God was upon him" (Luke 2:40). Grace meets *all* human needs; grace is patience, gentleness, tenderness, and compassion, and there is no circumstance that can arise where the abundance of God's grace is not available to everyone. This indeed feeds famished or starved affections and enriches life.

And forgive us our debts, as we forgive our debtors

And Love is reflected in love

What actually are our debts? Is it possible that the only debt we owe our fellow man is to see him as he really is—not as sick, aging, sinning, but as God is seeing him, whole, upright, and free? When we refuse to accept the mortal concept of man and only acknowledge his perfect divine identity, we open the door for Love's forgiveness to flow into our lives and wipe away any sense of guilt or of condemnation of man as a mortal or a sinner.

And lead us not into temptation, but deliver us from evil

And God leadeth us not into temptation, but delivereth us from sin, disease, and death

Divine Love, God, would never lead His loved creation into temptation, but rather defends and keeps everyone from any suggestions of discord or distress. All temptation is just believing there is another creation, mind, or existence, except God. But reaffirming that His kingdom has come and that His will is being done obliterates the belief that there is another power at work.

For Thine is the kingdom, and the power, and the glory, forever

For God is infinite, all-power, all Life, Truth, Love, over all, and All

And so the prayer brings thought back full circle to God's allness, His infinite, eternal presence, and His unopposable power and will. Just think of it. "*Thine* is the kingdom"—it belongs to God, it is where we dwell as loved children. "*Thine* is . . . the power," the power by which we live, the power of good. So God is all that is going on anywhere. And "*Thine* is . . . the glory." The light and radiance of God's presence eliminate darkness, doubt, and fear, and reveal that in spite of what the material senses may claim, God *is* infinite, eternal, and ALL.

As we become more familiar with praying this prayer from a higher standpoint of "heaven-born aspiration and spiritual consciousness," we will find that it heals instantaneously with inspiration that is fresh and new every day. This is how Christ Jesus prayed, how he taught his followers to pray. And today, as in his time, it meets all human needs.

—Jill Gooding

THE READER PRAYS

Dear God, this is a sacred, selfless hour.
    May I be clothed with Christ's humility
And know Thine is the glory and the power.
    Not person but Thy likeness may men see.

I cannot fear when I am serving Thee
    That any evil power can do me wrong.
The desk—the very place I love to be—
    Is not a target but a fortress strong.

Lord, bless the ones who gather here today,
    Who reach out for the truth to make them free.
For each heart filled with suffering or dismay
    Must drop its burdens, healed while praising Thee.

I pray Thy voice and only Thine be heard
    That rings out with Thy love so clear and sweet
It gives the perfect meaning of Thy Word—
    For I, too, listen humbly at Thy feet.

—Grace K. Sticht

Real Security from Animal Magnetism

*A*nimal magnetism. What does it mean? Can it affect me? How can I protect myself from it?

First, animal magnetism is a generic term our Leader, Mrs. Eddy, gives to all evil, including whatever is unlike God. The term is really self-explanatory. Animal magnetism is a magnetic pull on the human consciousness that would drag thought down to the level of animal reactions.

Can this so-called magnetic force affect people? Only if they are ignorant of its method of operation and do not understand God's omnipotence. On the whole, Christian Scientists realize that evil is merely the belief in an opposition to God and must not be indulged in any form. The earnest student of this Science would never knowingly yield to animal magnetism. But evil is not always obvious. It appears to work in subtle ways to ensnare even the most earnest student, unless he is awake. Thus the importance of ferreting out evil's ways and protecting oneself from the snares of animal magnetism.

How does animal magnetism claim to operate? Before one can successfully answer that question, he must first come to grips with the most important fact Christian Science reveals about animal magnetism—that it has no power or reality! That's right. It has not one iota of power, not one bit of truth. Power and reality belong to God alone. There cannot be two bases of power and existence—one good, the other evil. If there were two, God would not be omnipotent and omnipresent.

God is Mind, the intelligent governing force of all creation. Mind's supreme intelligence could not create or even know a so-called force that would, if given credence, dispute Mind's own kingdom. No facet of animal magnetism has any more reality than that of a lie. In the words of Mrs. Eddy: "A lie has only one chance of successful deception,—to be accounted true" (*Unity of Good*, p. 17).

"Well, if that's so, I might as well quit reading this article," one might say. Or even, "If evil has no power, why are we taking time to discuss the methods of protecting me from nothing?" Such reactions to the nonpower and nonreality of evil are naive, and naiveté has no place in metaphysical logic.

Evil has no power and existence but *claims* that it does and that it can victimize mankind by its false claims.

The talking serpent in the Garden of Eden has long symbolized evil. Did the serpent in the allegory have the power to make Eve eat the forbidden fruit? No, but it did *suggest* to her that the fruit was desirable and something she might enjoy. It even suggested that God didn't know what He was talking about when He forbade eating the fruit from the tree of the knowledge of good and evil.

The important point to remember is that Eve ate her own fruit. She responded to the serpent's arguments, which in themselves had no power to destroy her. They were only suggestions. In a sense, Eve destroyed herself.

This modus operandi of the serpent has been the method of animal magnetism throughout the ages. Evil can only suggest to human consciousness; it has no power to put the suggestion into operation. A person does that himself and then pays the consequences.

The great question is, then, "How do I keep from responding to animal magnetism's suggestions?" The answer is profound, yet so simple: Strengthen your human weaknesses! Animal magnetism's method is always to attack one at one's weakest point. Notice in life how often disturbances come through the same channel. For example, if one has a tendency to gossip, note how many times troubles stem from talking too much. If one is sensitive, the attacks may seem to come through the personal sense of a touchy nature.

In Christian Science, the healing of human weakness goes far beyond turning a weak mortal into a strong mortal. Healing entails lifting one's concept of himself into the realm of spiritual reality—awakening to the fact that he is not a mortal at all. As one recognizes his true nature as God's own reflection, he begins to prove his invulnerability to evil's attack. He demonstrates that error doesn't know the real man, the spiritual idea of God. Error doesn't know where Spirit's idea dwells or what Spirit's idea does, because error is provably unreal in Science.

To redeem the unredeemed elements in one's thinking is the best defense against any form of evil. Our Master, Christ Jesus, defeated evil's most aggressive attacks by his own purity. He knew who he was: "I and my Father are one" (John 10:30). And he also knew where he was going: "I go to the Father" (John 16:16). This knowledge of Christ, his true spiritual selfhood, lifted him beyond evil's reach and enabled him to prove evil powerless and unreal. On the mount of temptation he rejected every suggestion the devil offered him. The devil couldn't cast Jesus down; like the serpent, evil could only suggest that Jesus cast himself down. There was nothing in the Saviour's Godlike thought to respond to evil suggestions, so he resisted all the temptations.

The Science of Christ not only teaches how to recognize unredeemed facets of one's own life, it explains how to heal them. Self-knowledge is the first step in redemption. Taking an honest inventory of one's self shows the strong, Christly qualities one possesses, as well as the ungodlike traits that lead to trouble.

Ungodlike thinking and acting are eliminated by lifting one's concept of himself to his true being as God's likeness. Because man is God's reflection, he has always been expressive of the original—pure, sinless, whole. As one sees his spiritual innocence in Christ, the true idea, he progressively destroys the false beliefs that say he has ever lost this purity.

If error does seem to attack through some form of sin or disease, the alert metaphysician claims his innocence and purity in Christ, confident that Truth will uncover where the "leak" in security has taken place. A friend once told me that the water pressuring a dike had no intelligence to know where a hole was. But it was the nature of the force of the water to break through at the weakest spot, if there was one.

And so it is with animal magnetism. It does not have the intelligence to know anyone's weakness. But the nature of evil is to pressure the individual with aggressive mental suggestions. The yielding always comes through the avenue of the unredeemed human self—the self the Christ-idea must ultimately redeem.

Mrs. Eddy knew the inherent necessity for Christian Scientists to protect themselves from the aggressive suggestions of animal magnetism. In the By-Law in the *Manual of The Mother Church*

entitled "Alertness to Duty" she writes: "It shall be the duty of every member of this Church to defend himself daily against aggressive mental suggestion, and not be made to forget nor to neglect his duty to God, to his Leader, and to mankind. By his works he shall be judged,—and justified or condemned" (*Manual* Art. VIII, Sect. 6).

Sometimes when malicious animal magnetism seems to be attacking an individual, even as it did the Master, it appears as if the evil is far more vicious than just a suggestion coming to one's own thought. Evil appears to act through people and things. But that is evil's nature—to seem real and personal, vicious and malicious, when it really has no power. Jesus' crucifixion was not due to animal magnetism suggesting itself to Jesus, but animal magnetism suggesting his destruction to his enemies. The weakness was in the thoughts of the Pharisees and Sadducees, not in Jesus. This weakness made them prime targets for evil's suggestion that they would be blessed by the destruction of Jesus. Their acquiescence made them believe that by destroying the Master they could destroy the Christ, Truth, that he represented.

Jesus' resurrection is ultimate proof that animal magnetism is never beyond one's ability to handle it as suggestion. Had Jesus personalized the attack—seen it as personal or persons—he could not have defeated it. Jesus knew the real enemy was not the priests or the people but animal magnetism. Thus our Master was able to overcome the animal magnetism that used his persecutors. His final prayer was, "Father, forgive them; for they know not what they do" (Luke 23:34).

Mrs. Eddy says: "Evil has no reality. It is neither person, place, nor thing, but is simply a belief, an illusion of material sense" (*Science and Health*, p. 71). Clearly, to overcome evil, one must quit thinking of evil persons, evil places, or evil things. All evil is nothing more than a suggestion that there is a so-called force opposed to God. But the spiritual fact is that animal magnetism is not only powerless, it's not even an entity or a momentary reality. Christian Scientists heal evil successfully when they understand their Leader's teachings in regard to animal magnetism.

The Christ is the antidote for any form of evil. Christ, Truth, is the real attractive force of the universe, which lifts human consciousness to God. The constant communication of God, the Christ, shuts out the aggressive suggestions of the carnal mind that would attempt to destroy one, were he not alert to its methods. Christ reveals the Science of man's relationship to God, and this Science refutes the lie that evil has power and reality, or that man can be separated from good through even a suggestion of a power opposed to God. Practicing the Science of Christ is one's real security from animal magnetism.

Regardless of what evil seems to present to human thinking, regardless of how vicious or personal it claims to be, one only need weigh this claim in the scale with the Christ, Truth, to see its nothingness. In all its pretension, animal magnetism is never more than an illusion. An illusion has no power to act—only to fool; and the consciousness filled with the Christ can't even be fooled. As one weighs Mind's intelligence, Spirit's substance, and Life's activities in the scale with any illusion, it's not hard to realize the power lies with God.

—*Joanne Shriver Leedom*

SAFETY

*O*ne of the greatest statements made in all time concerning safety is that found in the Scriptures in the ninety-first Psalm: "He that dwelleth in the secret place of the most High shall abide under the shadow of the Almighty."

The text of this Psalm goes on to speak of refuge and fortress, of deliverance from snare and pestilence and destruction. It declares that no plague shall come near the dwelling of him who makes God his habitation. Angels shall have charge over him, long life shall satisfy him, salvation shall be shown unto him—all because he has set his love upon the Almighty and dwells in His secret place, under His shadow.

The writer of the Psalm evidently knew much about the safety which accompanies prayerful habitation within divine Mind. Obviously this dwelling in "the secret place," the unity of man with God, is spiritually mental, something which comes through prayer and understanding and spiritual power, and is not a matter of place or circumstance or outward determination. Clearly these promises say that by reason of love for and obedience to divine law and precept, within the sheltering understanding of the omnipresence of God, safety is found.

The world, however, has not found that safety. The race of Adam believes in a material existence separated from God and naturally unsafe because of that separation. By its own nature, having finite beginning and inevitable ending, and having no savior within itself, the material belief of existence is unsafe. And while many Christians have had spiritual comfort and consolation and definite help in these Scriptural promises of safety, for the bulk of mankind that has been no sure bulwark against disaster.

Safety, then, must have its source in something higher than material causes and effects. Safety, to be effectual, not only must cover spiritual welfare and security in some future life, but must include all the conditions of present-day existence. Safety, to be practical, must protect the human body and human affairs, must include all conditions and circumstances. Christian Science is teaching mankind that this safety comes through gaining an understanding of the omnipresence of God as divine Mind; by holding to divine ideas, which are themselves safe, and which by their very nature must always establish and promote safety wherever they are entertained.

Safety is not merely a physical circumstance, but a condition of spiritual understanding. Safety is never inherent in matter, but is found in the operation of divine Mind, overcoming the hazards of mortal mind and matter. Christian Science reveals a safety which cleanses the individual consciousness of sin, preserves the body from sickness, harmonizes all human affairs. This security is expressed as mortals surrender their belief in mortality and come into the faithful reflection of the nature, the will, and the power of divine Mind.

The word "reflection" means much to the student of Christian Science. In *Science and Health with Key to the Scriptures* Mary Baker Eddy writes (pp. 300, 301), "God is revealed only in that which reflects Life, Truth, Love,—yea, which manifests God's attributes and power, even as the human likeness thrown upon the mirror, repeats the color, form, and action of the person in front of the mirror." The task of the Christian Scientist is to manifest "God's attributes and power" by reflecting, expressing, divine Mind, and this through a fidelity as steadfast as is that of the reflection in the mirror to its original. The Christian Scientist learns, also, to protect the integrity of spiritual reflection from the aggressions of the material senses, that he be not robbed of his conscious oneness with divine qualities. In this spiritual progress he does not take for granted carelessly or casually this profound truth of divine protection. He knows he must secure it by every possible sacrifice of materiality, of the false sense of self. He finds it as he finds the continuity of his true spiritual being in divine Mind, God.

A noteworthy incident, occurring a number of years ago and related in part at that time in the *Christian Science Sentinel,* testifies to the safety which even in extreme circumstances is provided by the application of Christian Science.

A young mining engineer, accompanied by his wife, both of them devoted students of Christian Science, went deep into a great forest in the northwest section of the United States to examine a mine. The day they arrived at their proposed camp they found themselves menaced by a forest fire of tremendous proportions, and were swiftly surrounded by it so that apparently there was no way of escape. For more than seven hours they, with five miners, battled with the flames, beating out the fire upon one another's clothing, going down to the ground many times for a breath of air, seeking the apparent places of least destruction in the seething furnace of a whole mountainside. During these hours the two Christian Scientists maintained without a break their unwavering declarations of the power and presence of God to save them; declaring that His presence went with them, that the real man and the real earth are spiritual, not material, and that no destructive force could touch them.

Finally, at a terrifying crisis which threatened to sweep them all away, the wife called to her husband: "Oh, let's despise the danger; God never made it! This would have to destroy God before it could destroy His reflection." They clung to that great metaphysical fact, consciously maintaining their stand in Spirit, as spiritual ideas, and rejoicing in their refuge in divine Love. They realized with thanksgiving that the real man, as God's image and likeness, is just as safe as God Himself, and they claimed that safety in that hour. They rose to acknowledge revelation as Christian Science has brought it to the world, and they saw the power of the spiritual idea subdue the danger. This supreme moment turned the situation. They knew their victory, and very shortly all found their way to the back of the fire through a long green, unburned path which the flames had passed around and left untouched.

These students in their extremity applied the revelation, through Christian Science, that spiritual man, as the likeness of God, as idea in divine Mind, is just as safe as is God. They saw clearly that according to the figure of the mirror, the original must be reached before the reflection can be touched. Their years of faithful study and practice of Christian Science had so spiritualized their thought that in the hour of threatened devastation they could become aware of man as God's reflection, and of the universe as spiritual. The tangible actuality of spiritual creation, safe within God's knowledge of His ideas, came to their comprehension as a saving angel.

This instance of inspired deliverance can encourage all to rely upon spiritual understanding for the safety so constantly needed. Spiritually undefended human goodness, in the dream of life in matter, is not secure. To surmount chance and disaster, such goodness must be consciously controlled and protected by the law of God. Seeking spiritual understanding means seeking safety. For the reflection of divine Mind brings into present human experience that which the Discoverer and Founder of Christian Science calls, on page 561 of *Science and Health*, "the human and divine coincidence;" brings into actual demonstration the unity of God and man as Mind and Mind's indestructible idea.

Mrs. Eddy has written on page 424 of *Science and Health*, "Under divine Providence there can be no accidents, since there is no room for imperfection in perfection." The word "accident" is usually associated with that which is misfortune or mishap, but according to the dictionaries it means any interference with regular law, order, or purpose. Therefore, a happening or circumstance or condition of any kind not conforming to the intent of the law of God, could, broadly speaking, be classified as accident. The faithful reflecting of divine Mind stands guard against these mortal irregularities as the refuge and fortress, the shield and buckler, the deliverance from snare and pestilence and destruction and plague which the Psalmist discerned in what he called "the secret place of the most High."

Not only understanding, but application and deportment enter into the question of demonstrating divinely established safety. If one is to experience safety, he must make concrete in his daily life the truth which is itself safe. The reflection of divine Mind must occupy one's thought consistently and be expressed accurately in correct conduct if it is to determine one's experience.

That which is concrete is "particular, as opposed to that which is abstract and general." It is too easy a matter sometimes for the follower of Christian Science to have his devotion to the truth, which he acknowledges, abstract and general rather than concrete or demonstrated. It is possible for him to believe in Christian Science and yet keep his business, his home, his affairs, apart, still managed by human opinions, desires, methods. But as the truth he perceives is brought concretely, demonstrably, into the affairs of the day, his safety is assured. All detail of daily living must be rescued from human domination and brought under the government of divine Principle if experience is to be held secure. Christian Science teaches its followers how to do this saving thing. As one dematerializes his own mental attitude about the world and all there is in it, he comes out of belief in danger into the consciousness of safety. By this spiritualization of his thinking he also helps to bring safety to others.

Thus it is recognized that safety does not happen. It is earned. It is realized through uniting thought with divine Mind. As the reflection of Mind is maintained in one's consciousness, the presence and power of divine Mind, which holds secure the divine idea, the likeness and image of God, operate to keep the present human experience safe. This is because spiritual reflection heals human thought of all the fears and dangers which would make one's life unsafe, fortifying it with scientific conviction of the unreality and powerlessness of evil, and the all-power of good.

The student of Christian Science does not boast of safety in his own strength. He depends not upon personal wisdom. Rather does he lean upon the revealed fact that man, as God's idea, cannot stray from the eternal security of God's knowledge of His creation. He enjoys the safety of this divine coexistence in the exact degree of his fidelity to his understanding of it. Clearly, this unity with divine Mind is "the secret place." It is the substance of Christian Science healing. For the realization of this unity every Christian Scientist strives. And though his beginnings may be small, wrought out in trial and patience, he knows that in the measure of his enlightened faith they do bring him assured spiritual dominion, for they link his consciousness of being with the source of all safety—omnipotence itself.

—*Blanche Hersey Hogue*

"THE SONG OF CHRISTIAN SCIENCE"

*H*ave you ever thought what a joyous thing song is? Mary Baker Eddy, the beloved Discoverer and Founder of Christian Science, writes in her *Message to The Mother Church for 1900* (p. 2), "The song of Christian Science is, 'Work—work—work—watch and pray.'" She does not say, "Toil—toil—toil—worry and fret," but, "Work." And she tells us this work is a song, not a breathless, frustrating, exhausting experience, but a song, an acknowledgment of God's all-presence, all-power, all-science, so joyous and strong and pure that it coincides with revelation and results in demonstration.

As we contemplate the opportunities and tasks which God appoints for us as Christian Scientists, let us ask ourselves what it really means to be a Christian Scientist. Indeed, there is no greater calling. It is not enough to be a businessman, a wife, a mother, a musician, or a lawyer who is a Christian Scientist. The demand of Principle is to be a Christian Scientist first and foremost, a Christian Scientist who is a businessman, a wife, a mother, and so on. And there is a vast difference! Christian Science can take no secondary place in our lives. To be a Christian Scientist twenty-four hours a day is a full-time career and will bring recognition and success into our every walk of life. But there are no shortcuts. Everything we do must be to glorify God, not to gratify self.

Being a Christian Scientist brings with it wonderful foresight, quick discernment. It requires us to recognize the true motive and discard the wrong. The real Christian Scientist makes every situation an occasion to demonstrate Christian Science, to prove the allness of good and the nothingness of evil.

There appears to be greater resistance to spirituality in the world today than there has ever been. Error is hating more as it feels the presence of Truth. But the Christian Scientist is not afraid. He demonstrates self-knowledge, knowledge of his true selfhood in the image of God, and knowledge of that which in his human sense of self needs to be corrected and expunged. And he accepts each challenge as an opportunity to glorify God as he demonstrates over sin, sickness, and death for himself and for the world.

The demand of the hour is that we shall dedicate ourselves to a deeper understanding of Christian Science. We have scarcely begun to touch the vastness of Truth contained in our textbooks—the Bible and *Science and Health with Key to the Scriptures* by Mrs. Eddy and her other works. The slightest divergence from Principle is a departure from Science. Therefore we must go to the pure fountainhead through these textbooks and in humility, gratitude, and love pray over them, pore over them, assimilate them.

Spiritual ideas constantly unfold. Spiritual understanding is never stereotyped. We cannot hold to preconceived limited views of Science but must let Truth unfold in increasing grandeur and might in our consciousness. We must remember, however, that accurate understanding is not gained from spurious papers or publications, whatever their source, which claim a higher revelation than is found in our Leader's published writings in their latest editions. The divine revelation contained in these writings is complete and final. The Master warned that the way is straight and narrow. Indeed, "the song of Christian Science is, 'Work—work—work—watch and pray.'" But underlying and accompanying this song are the glorious harmonies, the depths and overtones of spiritual being.

The Apostle Peter described the calling of a Christian Scientist when he said (I Pet. 2:9), "Ye are a chosen generation, a royal priesthood, an holy nation, a peculiar people; that ye should shew forth the praises of him who hath called you out of darkness into his marvellous light."

Mrs. Eddy in her wisdom defines the wrong as well as the right practice of Christian Science. Had she left her great discovery merely in terms of absolute Truth without uncovering the error that is deceiving mankind and showing us how to overcome it, her work would have been incomplete, and the movement she founded could not have stood. She enables us to recognize and to defend ourselves against the aggressive suggestions of evil working so subtly that they often appear as our own thinking.

In order to detect and handle malpractice it is necessary that we understand true practice. Right practice is based upon an understanding and utilization of divine law whereby are demonstrated the presence, power, and allness of the one Mind, God. In right practice there are not two powers, matter and Mind, but one alone, Mind.

Mrs. Eddy says in *Miscellaneous Writings* (p. 114): "Christian Scientists cannot watch too sedulously, or bar their doors too closely, or pray to God too fervently, for deliverance from the claims of evil. Thus doing, Scientists will silence evil suggestions, uncover their methods, and stop their hidden influence upon the lives of mortals." Working, watching, and praying in humility and love, we must root out the false and hold fast that which is good. It is not enough to do this occasionally. It must be *daily*. The Psalmist said (Ps. 42:8), "The Lord will command his lovingkindness in the daytime, and in the night [in the dark, dark hours] his song shall be with me."

Jesus met and mastered the same deceptive forces of evil that would tempt us, and he left his example as our guide. Matthew records that hardly had he emerged from the baptism, that wonderful experience which confirmed his divine sonship, when mortal mind led him into the wilderness. Forty days and forty nights he fasted—rejected material sense testimony. Three times the devil tempted him. The first suggestion was, If you are the Son of God, use your spiritual power to gratify the senses. But Jesus rebuked this.

The second suggestion was, If you are the Son of God, show your spiritual power in some materially spectacular way. But Jesus rebuked this. The third aggressive suggestion was, You have all this power; use it for self-aggrandizement. This time Jesus no longer argued with error; he summarily dismissed it with the command, "Get thee hence, Satan" (Matt. 4:10). Then "angels came and ministered unto him." Not once was he deceived into accepting any of these suggestions as his own thought. That is why he did not give in to temptation.

Luke records that on one occasion, while teaching in the synagogue, Jesus pointed to his ministry as the promised Messiah. Then his hearers rose up and thrust him out of the city, intending to cast him headlong over the brow of the hill. But his habitual watching and praying so identified him with spirituality that they could not even see him, and he, passing through their midst, went his way.

On another occasion they would have come to make him a king by force. But popularity did not deceive Jesus. He withdrew alone to a mountain. That is what we must do. Often after some spectacular healing or some violent onslaught of mortal mind, he went to a mountain apart to pray. This was his protection and the protection of his work. Jesus always protected his work.

In the shocking experience of the beheading of John the Baptist, Matthew tells us that when Jesus heard it he departed into a desert place. But the multitudes followed him, and right then and there he healed their sick and fed the five thousand. Then he sent the multitudes and his disciples away, and again he went to a mountain to pray. These instances, and many others, illustrate how Jesus handled evil, or animal magnetism, instead of letting it handle him. He always worked and watched and prayed. Prayer was his protection.

Our beloved Leader did the same. Through her biographies we learn of the many attacks of evil, the many vicissitudes through which she passed to establish the Cause of Christian Science and give us the revelation. Referring to one of the most severe of these trials, she points to the blessing it held. May we all have the grace to see in every attack of animal magnetism only a blessing!

In order that we may claim the blessing, our thought must be as spiritual and pure as hers. Unless our own thought barbs it, the mental arrow is harmless. Then our handling of animal magnetism must start with ourselves. It must begin with a humility, as well as a spiritual clear-sightedness, that is not only willing to discern and cast out the error in our own thought but that actually does this. While matter and evil and fear are real to us, while human ambition, personal gain, personal domination, hatred, sensuality, rivalry, and self-love are real to us, we are responding to animal magnetism, not overcoming it.

It was the pure spirituality of the Master's thought that was his protection and caused him to triumph. It was the unselfed spiritual love of his faithful follower, our beloved Leader, which enabled her to stand and triumph. With both of them, their ceaseless prayer was (Luke 22:42), "Not my will, but thine, be done."

Christian Scientists are the only people in the world who know how to handle evil—to reduce it to nothingness. And the constant effort of animal magnetism is to make them forget this, to put them to sleep, and to make them try to handle error through worldly weapons. We cannot overcome evil, whether in our personal affairs, in world conditions, or in our branch churches, by resorting to clubs and stones. The Christian Scientist overcomes evil through prayer.

Error is not always met through the first denial. We must pray daily for ourselves. How? First of all, through taking time for prayerful, quiet study. If we really want it, we shall make time, and then we shall find the pattern of our lives becoming so clarified that there is time.

In working for ourselves, we need to ponder deeply and earnestly what God is. We must learn to know Him, love Him, and recognize our unity with Him. We must claim the spiritual nature of our being. Then we shall detect and recognize as false whatever aggressive mental suggestion may try to argue to us, be it unemployment, discouragement, lack, loneliness, condemnation of ourselves or others; be it sensuality, lust, disease, or fear of death—any of the myriad lies of life in matter. We must grow in spirituality to the point where thought turns naturally to God and dwells in Him—when we waken in the night, when we go about our business in the day.

Our daily metaphysical work must never become a formula. Unfolding spiritual ideas are alive and fresh. We have seen how Jesus continually went apart to pray; Mrs. Eddy did the same; and their healing work was instantaneous. We must do so too. Spirituality is not secondary. It demands that we sacrifice something for it. The present feebleness of our demonstration of Christian Science shows what immense spiritual growth must take place in our thinking.

One point upon which Mrs. Eddy lays great stress is found on page 146 of *The First Church of Christ, Scientist, and Miscellany*. She says: "Christian Scientists hold as a vital point that the beliefs of mortals tip the scale of being, morally and physically, either in the right or in the wrong direction. Therefore a Christian Scientist never mentally or audibly takes the side of sin, disease, or death." She continues, "He lays his whole weight of thought, tongue, and pen in the divine scale of being—for health and holiness." Mortal mind is prone to think and talk on the wrong side of the question, but gossip and rehearsing error are no part of Christian Science. The Christian Scientist puts his whole weight on the side of God, Spirit, and he keeps "the song of Christian Science" ever within him.

The only healer is divine Love. Let us pray for this Love to inhabit our hearts. Our work in demonstrating Christian Science must be carried on with great love. We need love in our churches; love in our practice; love in ourselves. Nothing else heals; nothing else will feed the spiritual hunger, draw the stranger to our churches, and solve the world's problems.

Truly St. Paul wrote (II Cor. 10:4, 5), "(… the weapons of our warfare are not carnal, but mighty through God to the pulling down of strong holds;) casting down imaginations, and every high thing that exalteth itself against the knowledge of God, and bringing into captivity every thought to the obedience of Christ."

—*L. Ivimy Gwalter*

SUFFICIENCY

The cause—God—which has produced the spiritual universe must have infinite resources for the eternal existence of its perfect work, laws for its continual government, power everlastingly to perpetuate it. This cause must be inseparable from its product, infinitely intelligent concerning it, and flawless in the maintenance of it. There must be perfection, also, of effect, if there is to be a perfect whole. Moreover, perpetuity of creation implies the orderly control of undeviating divine Principle, God.

Well may we stand in awe before the majesty of divine Principle, the perfect One, within whom "is every embodiment of Life and Mind" (*Unity of Good*, by Mary Baker Eddy, p. 3), all law, action, and accomplishment. All the qualities of perfection are expressed throughout God's creation. Everywhere divinity's boundless quantity is available and God's impartial law operative.

This cause, which is the Principle of all real manifestation, forms only perfect identities. With undeviating constancy it imparts to these identities the qualities of divinity, and governs their individual and universal expression. Sufficiency of supply is an eternal quality of God, and this quality is available to all creation at all times. Divine qualities cannot be accumulated or stored by creation, but they are being constantly expressed. Sufficiency of resources is maintained throughout God's universe by the operation of divine law, and so is present and permanent everywhere. Sufficiency of supply is not cumulative; rather is it being constantly unfolded. Where the source is infinite there is continuous impartation, oneness of cause and effect, and no need for accumulation. If in the universe of God's creating it were necessary for any part of this creation to accumulate some of the qualities, or quantity, of true substance, it would imply the possibility of a time when there might be an absence of substance, or a stoppage of its functioning, against which creation must provide. But such is unthinkable, impossible.

Divine Principle possesses infinite spiritual ideas, whereby it is abundantly able to manifest perfect harmony. All the ideas in the spiritual universe declare the control of divinity. In God's plan, man, whether considered individually or collectively, cannot accumulate or corner any quantity of substance. He can neither manage nor mismanage it. He can only express and be blessed by it. So man lives, not to accumulate supply, but forever to express its omnipresent sufficiency. Divine Science interprets through all creation the ever-presence of perfect supply and perfect continuity of existence.

Spirit enables all real identities to live within Spirit's resources, which are infinite. No part of God's creation can ever come to a situation in which there is lack. This truth is provable by anyone who will accept it and lean wholly upon it. Humanity may claim this truth today and experience deliverance from its belief of burden by the realization and demonstration of it. The divine law of infinite sufficiency operates with scientific simplicity, so that the supplying of creation with constant harmony is never obstructed or involved. Hence, the individual divine right and liberty of action of each idea is forever intact. Awaking humanity, beholding these ways of God, loving and obeying them, begins to be blessed by them.

Error, lifting its voice in contradiction of Truth, erroneously says, Accumulation is the only way whereby men can be saved from disaster. If they do not accumulate material possessions, they will be helpless, hopeless failures. But there are countless ways by which that which has been saved can be utterly wiped out. What a person has saved may even become the very means of his downfall. Surely such arguments as these contain no indication of absolute law. They rather indicate that the struggle for material accumulation may be part of the belief of animal magnetism which Mrs. Eddy describes as "one belief preying upon another" (*Science and Health with Key to the Scriptures*, p. 583).

Opposed to this false belief stands the heavenly order of universal care, namely, the divine unfoldment of exhaustless resources. God has unlimited resources for His entire universe, and divine Science maintains the reflection of these resources throughout creation.

The foregoing statements, however, offer no excuse for humanity to be careless, extravagant, or thoughtless about what is humanly necessary and right to have. On the contrary, Christian Science teaches the application of these spiritual truths in human life through the exercise of wisdom, economy, and thoughtful provision for all intrusted to us by human circumstances. Spiritual understanding renders human thought more foreseeing, more prudent, more resourceful and alert. It causes all that is humanly done in accord with divine law to prosper and to abide so long as it is useful.

Right investment of one's means may be as necessary as the right care of one's clothes or one's home. But let us not put our trust in matter in any form or amount. Rather, let us administer wisely what comes to our hand and abide satisfied in the understanding that Spirit is man's only real source of supply. Man's coexistence with Spirit enables him to receive the comfort, freedom, and support of infinite resources. If our thinking is governed by spiritual truth, all that is part of our daily human affairs, whether animate or inanimate, will be governed by divine law, and so will work together for good to those who love God—Spirit.

As humanity gathers the facts of divine Life through communion with the one Mind, and forsakes the beliefs of mortality, this process will preserve all that is useful and good in human experience, and will cause the evidence of good to abide and expand until there is no belief or appearance of lack left to deny the allness and omnipresence of good. We shall have more to share by gaining spiritual understanding, and using it in demonstration, than we can possibly have by accumulating matter.

Mrs. Eddy's life was a marvelous example of this truth. As she gave her whole life to the purpose of knowing God, for the sake of helping humanity, she became rich in spiritual substance; and this was necessarily outlined in her human condition. As she gained the treasure of divine wisdom there accumulated a wealth of spiritual supply for her, and through her for the world. Mrs. Eddy writes on page 319 of *Science and Health,* "To calculate one's life-prospects from a material basis, would infringe upon spiritual law and misguide human hope." She has taught us by precept and practice that Mind alone is the Giver of all good to man. This spiritual fact is closely related to humanity's progress from sense to Soul.

Jesus had such a realization of immediate divine help available for present human need that he said: "Thinkest thou that I cannot now pray to my Father, and he shall presently give me more than twelve legions of angels?" (Matt. 26:53.) May not this statement be taken as indicating that prayer to God, or the communing with the spiritual truths of being, is the means for humanity's deliverance from the sense of lack in every direction?

A familiar Bible story proves that the recognition of the spiritual law of divine substance, when applied in daily human life, solves its perplexing problems. It is the story of the widow and her sons and her pot of oil, which is told in II Kings 4:1–7. Material sense, regarding the condition of poverty outlined in these verses, might have said: There are not enough resources in this family, so there must follow discord, disgrace, and sorrow. There is no solution for the problem. There has been no accumulation of matter, so there must be a time of punishment. Everything must express lack: the oil, lack of quantity; the woman, lack of faith and resources; the sons, lack of freedom; and the creditors, lack of payment.

But a prophet entered into the case. In *Science and Health* (p. 593) "prophet" is defined as "a spiritual seer; disappearance of material sense before the conscious facts of spiritual Truth." Elisha, the prophet, looked at the widow's case through spiritual sense, and he must have seen sufficiency as a quality of ever present Life. Immediately the oil manifested sufficiency instead of limitation; the sons expressed assurance of freedom instead of fear of slavery; the creditors expressed satisfaction instead of deprivation; and the woman possessed further resources instead of poverty.

No time for the accumulation of matter was required. Mind was the multiplier, and sufficiency was made manifest even in the material realm, so called. The false material sense gave way to the spiritual fact of Truth. Everything in the case, animate and inanimate, came into obedience to the law of God. Elisha's clear sense brought forth increased evidence of the exhaustless nature of true supply. He demonstrated the power of spiritual truth in the human problem. It is through such an example as this that thought is led to recognize, in every situation that it is not the amount of material possessions which makes it possible for sufficiency to be expressed, but the understanding that sufficiency of good is a divine quality forever present and maintained by divine law; and this, in spite of how much, or how little, of matter seems to be present.

These truths are available for every human being to demonstrate. They can waken him to the realization that his situation is not hopeless, his burden not heavy, his poverty not real, his riches not uncertain, his possessions not fluctuating. In proportion as he understands and uses the spiritual facts of real substance, the good he gains is protected and preserved to him. Thus he will finally learn that God's divine method of impartation, and man's spiritual ability to receive what comes from God, is the law whereby creation remains perfect.

Thus so-called human life will become an ever increasing experience of awareness of the presence of divine truth. And soon there will begin to ring in the hearts of men the unbroken rhythm of the heavenly melody, "My grace is sufficient for thee" (II Cor. 12:9).

—*Julia M. Johnston*

Supply—and Going Into the Public Practice of Christian Science

A number of years ago I had entered the public practice of Christian Science and was frequently afraid I wasn't going to be able to pay the family bills. We had no savings; one child was in grade school and one was entering junior high; we had a mortgage, food and utility expenses, and several thousand dollars of debt incurred prior to my going into the practice.

Every time an envelope containing a bill arrived in the mail I became afraid. Often I would simply put these envelopes into my desk drawer, hoping that they could be put off until a better time.

One night, about one o'clock, I woke from sleep greatly distressed about finances. I went to the drawer containing all the unopened bills and sorted through them. There were many duplicates, many first and second notices from utility companies, and, to my dismay, a third notice on our water bill. In fact, our water service was to be cut off at eight o'clock that very morning if the bill was not paid. I looked at the amount; we had just enough in the checking account to pay it. But there was resistance to using the money because fear kept telling me if I did, I wouldn't have anything left.

I overcame this resistance, jumped in our car, and raced over to the water company office. I deposited the envelope containing our payment in the night depository. I wrote on the envelope in big red letters, "Our payment is enclosed. Please do not shut off our water service."

Back home I vowed I would never again let fear keep me from facing up to responsibility. I would never again let fear suggest that I do to myself what fear on its own did not have the power to do to me—take away my innocence, wisdom, and love as one of God's children.

I spent the next few hours going through all of our unopened mail. I threw out duplicate billings, prioritized the remainder of them, and then prayed to remove the fear of inability to meet these obligations. I asked myself, "Can God be lacking in anything? If lack isn't part of God's existence, could He, in all fairness, create His own children subject to lack? As one of God's children, can I ever find myself in a position where I do not have the practical means to prove that lack cannot control my existence?"

As I prayed for understanding and guidance to know how to approach my finances now that I wasn't receiving a specific salary, I found there were basic truths about God that (far from being cold, impracticable statements) were warm, loving provisions available to help me right where I was that morning. For instance:
- God is One—He is not competing with Himself;
- God is infinite—without beginning or end;
- God is Mind—wisdom and intelligence.

What I understood of God's oneness enabled me to see that there aren't two universes—the spiritual one and the one where I seemed to be at the moment. There is only the spiritual one, which is God's. And the more clearly we understand God as divine Principle and trust Him because of this understanding, the more we see God's reign of goodness and justice.

I also saw that His universe is not based on having to choose between competing alternatives. Each aspect of God's creation must have value. Each must have provision for its existence. This existence is not skimpy but complete; it is not dependent upon having another part of creation give up part of its place and provision. Humanly speaking, then, I could expect all of my bills to be paid.

The infinitude of God's love showed me that spiritual supply—the basis for what we perceive as having our needs met—has its foundation in an unlimited God. Whatever is needed to keep the spiritual universe forever in balance is available without any possibility that it will wear out or diminish. The means to pay my bills had to be there. It did not stop when I ceased getting a paycheck.

The fact that God is Mind allowed me to know there is no waste in His universe. Indeed there is abundance. Wisdom and intelligence would dictate, however, that it is an abundance that fully meets a need, not an abundance that allows for extravagance or misuse. With this understanding I felt better able to distinguish between legitimate needs and selfish wants.

I also began to see that just as God is my source of supply, so is He the source of supply for all of my creditors. This was not an attempt to escape rightful obligation but rather the removal of a false sense of responsibility so that I could keep my thought centered on what is true spiritually.

That morning was the turning point for me in our demonstration of supply. Things didn't change overnight, but they did change. During the next few years we became current in our bills, and the sizable indebtedness was completely eliminated.

It became important during that period to know that my family and I were not second-class citizens because we had decided to trust in God. How could we be victimized by being obedient to the central teaching of the Bible that says God is above all, that God is good, and that God is the source of all good?

"There is therefore now no condemnation to them which are in Christ Jesus, who walk not after the flesh, but after the Spirit. For the law of the Spirit of life in Christ Jesus hath made me free from the law of sin and death" (Rom. 8:1, 2). These verses from Romans became a staff upon which I leaned many times.

Over the next several days, as I prayed to understand more about dignity, it came to me to write to our creditors and share with them what I was doing—to explain that I was in no way trying to get out of paying each one of them in full. I was surprised at the response. There were a few computer-generated letters, but there were also real letters and telephone calls from individuals expressing understanding and support and offering assistance in whatever way each could. I began to see something of the completeness of God's universe working as a coordinated whole. The lie of loss of dignity and integrity began to fall away, and progress became even more rapid.

I found the biggest help during this period was to examine my thought consistently. Every time a suggestion of poverty, injustice, victimization, or futility presented itself to me, I immediately took the time to correct such ungodlike thoughts. I prayed to understand more clearly that what had to be true of God was therefore also true of His image and likeness, man—which was and is my true identity. If mortal reasoning said I had the time to contemplate an ungodlike suggestion, I knew I had time to correct it with the truth of God—no matter where I was or what I was doing.

I began to sense that, spiritually, supply and demand are always in balance. They are two ways of looking at the same thing: the reality of God. God is! This can be equated to supply. God can't help being what He is! This can be equated to demand. God is Love. Love can't help being loving. Love, and Love's loving, are always in balance.

Since spiritual man is the full representation of God, Soul, I began to catch glimpses of how man relates to this balance of supply and demand. Spiritually, man's supply must be the provision of everything that makes man God's complete representative. I saw that when the argument of lack screamed its loudest, I needed to understand that I was already God's complete expression. I needed to see that this truth translated into practical government of my financial affairs right here, right now. It was clear that my Father-Mother God needed me to be a *correct* witness of Him. "God gives you His spiritual ideas, and in turn, they give you daily supplies," writes Mrs. Eddy (*Miscellaneous Writings*, p. 307).

As I understood this, the means for our family to eat properly and to be clothed, to begin paying our bills, and to hold on to our home began to appear. Sometimes the answer was through something we were led to do. At other times, as I learned to discard false pride and ego, help came through the provision of a loving neighbor, friend, or church member.

During this period of spiritual growth, I also found there were numerous misunderstandings about supply and the human appearance of supply that needed to be corrected.

For instance, I found that supply and fear do not work together. It may be right to have a savings account or an investment or retirement account; but such management of supply should never have as its reason a fear that God won't be there tomorrow to meet our needs.

This was one of the lessons the children of Israel had to learn as they began their journey in the wilderness after Moses brought them out of bondage (see Ex. 16:11–21). There was the need to learn to depend upon God moment by moment. The Israelites couldn't store up the quails or the manna. They had to trust that God was going to provide for them in the evening and the following morning just as He had provided for them each previous evening and morning. Wisdom, not fear that God won't be there tomorrow or next year, should be the basis for proper management of our finances.

Also, I needed to ensure that I didn't inadvertently begin trusting in income from the practice, investments, or government benefits, when I should be trusting God alone. God is always the source of all that is real and good. Money, no matter what its source, is simply a symbol of God's provision for us.

Another ignorant thought about supply I had to be sure I didn't succumb to was that it is going to appear like magic. Of course it's not a question of expecting a money-bearing tree to appear on my front lawn! I certainly couldn't passively sit back either and expect to be supplied for doing nothing. I had to be actively working up to my highest ability—in my case, expressing my understanding of God through the practice of Christian Science—in order to see the provision of God operate.

While the human appearance of supply may often take the form of money, I also needed to be alert not to fall into the habit of seeing supply only in the form of money. I saw that by trusting mortal reasoning instead of God, by outlining the solution I thought was correct, by bowing down to pride or a false sense of responsibility, I would be limiting the application of spiritual laws to a problem and thereby be blinded to some divinely inspired solution that would meet our needs much better than anything I could humanly foresee. I needed to remember that supply also has its human appearance in the form of food, clothing, shelter, scholarships, grants, gifts, barter, and so many other means.

The last major misunderstanding that fell away during this period was the subtle argument that says the amount of our material possessions is an indication of the relative value of God's love for us—he who has more is loved more; or he who has more understands more.

God's love is shared equally by all of His creation; therefore, the relative term more (or *less*) has no meaning in spiritual consciousness. Each of us, as a complete idea reflecting the one God, has what that one God has—none more, none less. Age, family background, educational experience, and geographical location are not factors in demonstrating the spiritual laws of God.

In *Miscellaneous Writings* Mrs. Eddy writes: "God is universal; confined to no spot, defined by no dogma, appropriated by no sect. Not more

to one than to all, is God demonstrable as divine Life, Truth, and Love; and His people are they that reflect Him—that reflect Love.... He guards, guides, feeds, and folds the sheep of His pasture; and their ears are attuned to His call" (pp. 150–151).

Our water service was not turned off that morning several years ago. But I have found that I can't afford to lapse into a false sense of security as if I had "made my demonstration of supply." Supply is one of those concepts that doesn't lend itself to a one-time demonstration. It is so vast in its implications that we need to work with it and deepen our understanding of its source daily.

—*Timothy A. MacDonald*

THE TALENT THAT HEALS

*T*here is a fable that a small spider was accidentally shut in the back of a watch. Its position appeared hopeless. But it did the one thing a spider can do. It spun a web. And that gummed up the works! The watch was opened for cleaning, and the spider was free. He was free because he used the special talent a spider has.

We also have a talent. Everybody has it. It is the most powerful talent there is. There is absolutely nothing it cannot achieve. But it needs developing. It is the talent to love.

Man has this talent because he is God-created, and because God is Love itself. It is as natural for us to love as for spiders to spin webs. A baby loves as it clutches at the beads around your neck and smiles up at you. A schoolboy loves as he shares his dinner with his dog. Parents love as they ponder their children's welfare.

But love has deeper depths, wider outreach. Pure love is totally unselfed, vitally intelligent, since Love is also Mind. As we develop more of this unselfed love, we find ourselves spontaneously healing.

Only unselfed love brings a Christian Science treatment to life. Mrs. Eddy declares, "By the truthful arguments you employ, and especially by the spirit of Truth and Love which you entertain, you will heal the sick" (*Science and Health*, p. 418).

Unselfed love has no element of personal attachment. It is the reflection of that divine Love which recognizes nothing but Love's allness—no sin, sorrow, disease, or death. Such love is humanly expressed on two levels—the moral, or ethical, and the spiritual.

On the moral, or ethical, level we must have enough unselfed love to respond both to the spoken and unspoken plea for help, at whatever inconvenience to ourselves.

"Somebody hath touched me" (Luke 8:46), said Christ Jesus, sensing the unspoken appeal of the sick woman in the throng as people jostled about him when he was on his way in answer to the call to heal Jairus' daughter. He responded to the silent reaching out of the unknown woman before going on to what humanly appeared to be a more urgent and more important case.

Acting with unselfed love on a moral and ethical level, the practitioner visits the cases that need visiting, goes the second mile, is conscientious in the treatments given, is patient with the impatient. Through the Christ this selfless love brings the Father's love to humanity in ways humanity can appreciate.

But what of unselfed love on a deeper, more spiritual level? "For their sakes I sanctify myself," said Jesus, praying for his disciples, "that they also might be sanctified through the truth" (John 17:19). Mrs. Eddy points to the need for similar self-abnegation: "The true understanding of Christian Science Mind-healing never originated in pride, rivalry, or the deification of self." And further: "The ways of Christianity have not changed. Meekness, selflessness, and love are the paths of His testimony and the footsteps of His flock" (*Rudimental Divine Science*, p. 17).

Do we pray for love enough to follow these directives? They can show us the way, but we must walk it ourselves. Love makes deep and continuing demands on us to develop this talent to the point of healing. Yielding to these demands, we feel the unsurpassed reward of the Father's blessing.

To love so is to dig deep into the divine metaphysics of Christian Science, to explore the Bible and Mrs. Eddy's writings, to follow her in her discovery and join in the love and gratitude she expresses in these lines from her poem "The New Century":

> Dear God! how great, how good Thou art
> To heal humanity's sore heart;
> To probe the wound, then pour the balm—
> A life perfected, strong and calm.
> (*Poems*, p. 22)

To love is to abandon, at whatever cost and through however much struggle, whatever in us is unlike the healing Christ, and to claim our true and Christly selfhood, however much the devil may seem to mock and frustrate our efforts. Such love heals. It heals ourselves and others.

The unselfed love we bring to a patient enables us to discern his need. His need may not always be what it appears to be. The patient himself may not always be aware of his own need.

A practitioner was rung up one evening by a frightened young man whose wife had been taken suddenly ill, losing the use of her limbs. The practitioner was already occupied with some very pressing work, and as the couple were at a distance, she suggested they get help locally. This they were unable to do, and at this point the practitioner realized there was no finity to loving. She willingly accepted the case.

She began by denying the physical symptoms and replacing them with the perfect concept of the spiritual activity of all God's ideas. But as her love reached deeper, she became aware of the real need. She remembered that whenever this young man wrote her he said what a support his wife was to him. With a flash of illumination it occurred to her that a support is something which has to bear another weight, and might eventually collapse under the strain. Searching for the counterfact—the truth of the situation—she saw it lay in the idea of partnership.

Far into the night she worked to establish in her own thought the lovely spiritual fact that the children of God, being equal, are engaged in a partnership. In the morning she was not surprised, though she was humbly grateful, to learn that the young wife was well and about her normal activities.

As we develop our talent for unselfed love, spiritual discernment becomes more acute, and healing more certain.

Unselfed love never blames the patient for lack of healing. It never pleads an ungrateful patient but gets busy knowing there is no such thing as ingratitude.

Unselfed love never boasts of its healing work or suffers from wounded pride or discouragement if healing is not quickly manifest. It never dictates, advises, demands. On the other hand, it is not afraid to risk displeasure by giving timely warnings. It will "probe the wound" as well as "pour the balm," not in a personal way that can hurt, but by reflection of the Love that is God.

We can take this precious talent—this talent for loving that divine Love bestows upon each one of us—and develop it to our fullest spiritual understanding. And with loving expectancy we can trust that spiritual understanding to deepen with each successive day.

—*Rosemary Cobham*

TEN GOOD LAWYERS

*I*t had been a pretty unsettling couple of weeks, to say the least. It was obvious to me that I had symptoms associated with breast cancer. I did not go for a medical diagnosis, because I've always found that turning to God in prayer has brought healing, even in the most threatening situations. Now, immobilized by tremendous fear, I prayed first for the calm simply to *pray*.

One afternoon, I was sitting in my study, where I often spend time praying. I was reading from *Miscellaneous Writings* by Mary Baker Eddy. My eyes were following the words—and they were good, reassuring, even healing, words—but I was preoccupied with a constant, nagging dread. Then something very soft and urgent tugged at my thought. It was like a faint whisper: "Why don't you get down on your knees and pray?"

I dismissed the idea and kept reading. Again it came. "Why don't you just get down on your knees and pray?"

After resisting it a few more times, I thought, "Well, OK." I closed the book and bowed down and prayed with all my heart. "Father, help me," I pleaded. "I feel like I need ten good lawyers!"

I don't often think in terms of lawyers, but I was in no position to question the form of the prayer that was coming to me. And immediately I heard a most tender message: "I have given you ten good lawyers." Then, even while these words were repeating themselves, my hand reached for my Bible, and it opened to Exodus, chapter 20. This is what I read: "And God spake all these words, saying, I am the Lord thy God, which have brought thee out of the land of Egypt, out of the house of bondage" (verses 1, 2).

I knew that God had spoken these words directly to Moses and that they had divine authority. This wasn't just a promise for future deliverance, but an assurance that deliverance has already taken place for any circumstance that might arise. The bondage I felt to fear, disease, and doom started to lose its grip on me. This was encouraging. I was seeing something of God's care and shepherding. God loves us. He has already tenderly led us out of darkness and enslavement. God has liberated all of us from anything that would inhibit our natural witness of Him. Each of the Ten Commandments argues on our behalf. Each insists on our innate innocence as God's beloved. Accepted and lived in daily life, these divine truths are enough to counter all the terrors of mortal existence.

I. Thou shalt have no other gods before me. God is the only God. Nothing could replace God, pretend to be God, or overshadow or threaten God. I could see that, in my case, the "other gods" were fear, disease, and death. But in the allness or "onlyness" of God, there could be no other power called disease, no other power called death. God is Life, and Life is ever-present good. *All* good. I understood disease to be an imposter, making itself a god to be worshiped, and undermining faith in the one and only God. I saw the impossibility of dividing my allegiance to God with "other gods." For me, it became a question of faithfulness.

II. Thou shalt not make unto thee any graven image, or any likeness of any thing that is in heaven above, or that is in the earth beneath, or that is in the water under the earth: Thou shalt not bow down thyself to them, nor serve them . . . . I am not a maker, I thought. God is *the* Maker. This commandment made plain to me that God created all that exists, and that this creation is complete. *Graven* can mean something that is pressed into, or fixed indelibly on, the memory. This commandment gave me the ability to dismiss false impressions—made by imagination or fear, or produced by the media or evolved from conversations I'd heard. God's children are not helpless victims of random and cruel evil. As the direct outcome of divine Mind, I could only be impressed by the good that comes from this Mind. This meant that while I could be in awe of God's love and kindness, I didn't need to be impressed by an opposite to God called evil. I could delight in God's creation. His creations are wholly good. Disease is unlike God, and I could not be made, through fear, to "bow down" or to serve false images of disease and death by believing them, by allowing them to flourish in my thought, or by letting them dictate my behavior. I could choose to worship the only Love, by fearless faithfulness and by trusting God to care for me and to be my Physician.

III. Thou shalt not take the name of the Lord thy God in vain; for the Lord will not hold him guiltless that taketh his name in vain. What is God's name? I thoroughly pondered the synonyms, or names, for God that I had found in the Bible and in reading *Science and Health* over the years. I knew some of God's names to be *Life*, *Truth*, and *Love*. We express Life in living, Truth in integrity, Love in affection. Another of the names for God is *Soul*, which we bear witness to in goodness and in beauty. God is *Spirit*, which means we are wholly spiritual and vital.

God is *Mind*, which is expressed in calm and in wisdom. Divine wisdom assures that since God is all-powerful and all-knowing, there is no power but Him, and nothing to know but good. God is Principle, and this Principle is expressed in divine order and perfection. The disorder and chaos of disease is not from God. My deep desire not to take the Lord's name in vain helped me to reason that the name of cancer, or the name of any disease had to be a lie about God, an attempt to take away His name or distort His nature. God's name, the nature of good, is present and permanent.

IV. Remember the sabbath day, to keep it holy. ...For in six days the Lord made heaven and earth, the sea, and all that in them is, and rested the seventh day: wherefore the Lord blessed the sabbath day, and hallowed it. Every day belongs to God. Every day is filled with the activity of God, and therefore there is no day in which evil begins or reigns. There is no day that is given over to disease and dismay. There is no starting point for evil. Each day is holy, heavenly. Disease has no "move-in date," no beginning or origin. This commandment reconfirms God's creative power. He made all. There is nothing more to be made, nothing more to create, to grow, or to develop. God's creation is complete, finished, and blessed.

V. Honour thy father and thy mother: that thy days may be long upon the land which the Lord thy God giveth thee. God is Father-Mother of all that is—the divine Parent. There is no creation or child of God called disease. God's ideas are pure and good and have the eternal life that God gives. This is our heritage, the "land" that we possess. The honoring of divine Life gives us eternal life, and this is God's gift to all.

VI. Thou shalt not kill. God-given happiness and existence cannot be killed or deadened by fear or the threat of disease. The Christ—the awareness of God as the presence of good—cannot be snuffed out. God, Spirit, enlivens us and gives us vitality and health. We are not suddenly, or gradually, separated from God. His intention for us is that we live—that we actively express Life here and now.

A psalm reminds us, "I shall not die, but live, and declare the works of the Lord" (Ps. 118:17).

VII. Thou shalt not commit adultery. Beliefs about the inevitability of disease and death cannot seep in to contaminate God's pure creation. It is essential to defend our thinking from sickening mortal influences, by keeping it aligned with goodness, with God. We have a divine right to refuse admittance to invasive evil. Such a right is preserved through prayer. When we ask God how we are, the answer comes as kind reassurance that we are His beloved. We are whole and well and safe. We do not hurt or cause hurt. We are not overly sensitive, fragile, insensitive, or hard. We are Godlike. We are defined by balance, kindness, spiritual evenness, and poise. Matter and its various states do not define us as spiritual beings. Women are not helpless, vulnerable, or weak. As God's daughters, they are strong, divinely protected, able to arm themselves with spiritual truth through deep, trusting communion with divine consciousness.

VIII. Thou shalt not steal. Nothing given to us by God can be taken away. Our God-given possessions are life, happiness, freedom, peace, and a sense of well-being—of *being* well. I reasoned that I could not be robbed of my innocence, the Christly view of safely coexisting with God, protected by divine and ever-present Love. I saw that my confidence in God as my lens, my substance, and the source of my condition is a permanent possession.

IX. Thou shalt not bear false witness against thy neighbour. Every one of God's children has the right to claim immunity from cruel beliefs. Women, God's daughters, are not maligned victims. Likewise, the sons of God deserve to be identified as Godlike, and free from enslaving traits and actions. God's sons are gentle and peace-loving. To believe that anyone in God's creation could be an afflicter, or afflicted, would be to break this commandment. Each one is safe in God's care and responsive to His thoughts and directions. To have true affection for my neighbor is to see my neighbor as God's cherished and perfect child—to bear spiritually accurate witness.

X. Thou shalt not covet thy neighbour's house, thou shalt not covet thy neighbour's wife, nor his manservant, nor his maidservant, nor his ox, nor his ass, nor any thing that is thy neighbour's. There is no tendency to covet when we understand spiritually that we have all good now, and that one cannot possess the substance of any good that someone else does not have, including health. One individual does not possess calm, and another not. One does not have joy or clear consciousness, and another not, and so on. God's goodness is freely bestowed on all. Everyone is included in God's love. There are no have-nots in the kingdom of God, and that is where we are living, *now*.

This concluded my prayer. I looked up at the clock, and just a little more than an hour had gone by. And yet everything had changed. God had worked on me, and in me, and had won me over. I felt fearless. The physical threat no longer mattered to me. God's laws had come alive in my thinking and had ministered to me. My case had been argued by ten good lawyers, and they had won my release.

Over the next few days the symptoms disappeared completely, and they have not returned. The transformation in my thought since that time, though, is still resonating. I felt touched by a loving, clearly enunciated divine presence that would never let me go. And what I love about this experience is that I know it is not mine alone, but that it belongs to everyone, under the laws of God. Everyone has ten brilliant lawyers working for them all the time.

—*Rebecca Odegaard*

THE THEOLOGY OF CARE

The traditional Christian standard of care rests on Christ Jesus' parable of the good Samaritan. The parable's message provides a theological basis for supplying physical care to one in need. The lawyer whose questions elicited Jesus' illustration had summarized the way to obtain eternal life by quoting the Mosaic law: "Thou shalt love the Lord thy God with all thy heart, and with all thy soul, and with all thy strength, and with all thy mind; and thy neighbour as thyself." Jesus approved this statement.

Then, in answer to the lawyer's question, "... who is my neighbour?" the Master presented the parable of the good Samaritan (see Luke 10:25–37). But from his approval of the lawyer's summary, it should be clear that obedience to the second command—loving our neighbor—logically requires obedience to the first—loving God. The Christian ministry of care rests on divine help. Through our worship of God we receive spiritual sustenance and gain the strength to aid another.

In God's perfect creation, harmony is perpetual. God's care is His own perfect loving of all that He has made, providing infinite good. The spiritual understanding of divine Love calls forth human aid that is imbued with the power of God.

All need for human assistance is temporary. The fundamental truth of man's individual, spiritual completeness includes the fact that in reality each of us is dependent on God, not on each other. And we can all turn to God for help and receive it. Mrs. Eddy tells us: "No one can save himself without God's help, and God will help each man who performs his own part. After this manner and in no other way is every man cared for and blessed" (*Retrospection and Introspection*, p. 86).

Christ Jesus loved his neighbor. After describing the simple setting for his series of lessons known as the Sermon on the Mount, Mrs. Eddy says, "In this simplicity, and with such fidelity, we see Jesus ministering to the spiritual needs of all who placed themselves under his care, always leading them into the divine order, under the sway of his own perfect understanding" (*Retrospection and Introspection*, p. 91). What Jesus did for his fellowman was tangible, but distinctly and thoroughly spiritual. His efforts met the human need; those who sought his help were healed, and those who received his teaching were saved. Jesus proved that our needs are actually spiritual, not material, and that God, Spirit, supplies the spiritual sustenance to satisfy one completely. He lived his own parable of the good Samaritan.

Jesus' spirituality governed his human life conclusively; it enabled him to show the nature of God's love. He taught and lived the Christ. Even in the presence of discord he knew what was true, and through his spiritual understanding he demonstrated the supremacy of God, annulling the mortal sense. This understanding still provides spiritual care just as it did in Jesus' ministry. This is evidence of God's care for us. No inadequacy, mistake, or failure exists in this divine provision. No construction of mortal belief has the capacity to resist the Christ.

The Master's ministry of care included healing, but that care was also manifest in his teaching and preaching. Today the activities of the Church of Christ, Scientist, provide the same complete ministry. Every Church function established by Mrs. Eddy in the *Manual of The Mother Church* is a care activity, including the Bible Lessons (in the *Christian Science Quarterly*), church services, Christian Science Reading Rooms, class instruction, public lectures, and the work of The Christian Science Publishing Society. And we receive care in its most individualized form through the aid provided by Christian Science practitioners and nurses.

Care, as an expression of divine Love, does not omit proper care for ourselves, and this begins with taking good care of our thinking—no frivolous task. Each new day takes form out of the action of thought. What thoughts will we think? What concepts of life do we honor? Beginning the day with prayer, including study of the Bible and the Christian Science textbook, *Science and Health* by Mrs. Eddy, we gain and maintain the inspired comprehension of our oneness with God. Then the demands we face are carried out with spiritual enlightenment, and we are less likely to be influenced by materialism.

Spiritual understanding enables us to recognize God's ever-present care, but this understanding requires cultivation. When our thought manifests thorough spiritual preparation, everything we need in order to take good care of ourselves will come in natural order.

Another aspect of care is the charge to love our neighbor as ourselves. Paul considered the members of the Church as one body in Christ. He said, "God hath tempered the body together, having given more abundant honour to that part which lacked: that there should be no schism in the body; but that the members should have the same care one for another" (I Cor. 12:24, 25).

The individual who requests the services of a Christian Science nurse is approaching his human need from a spiritual standpoint. Physical care provided in harmony with the patient's theology supports his spiritual growth, while at the same time supporting the practitioner's treatment. Christian Science nursing demands the capacity and skill that come with solid spiritual development, thorough training, and dedicated practice. Christian Science nursing care closes the gap between what the patient needs to have done and what he is able to do for himself—*until* he is able to do it for himself.

The mortal sense of existence holds to a different concept of care. Human emotions and sensations insist that one's primary need is for physical change, or improvement, and that spiritual requirements are secondary or even impossible to fulfill in the face of physical discord. If one submits to these assertions, he places himself under the domination of materiality. Then efforts to render assistance are hemmed in by mortality, and anxiety drains one's resources. To experience genuine comfort and healing, the individual needs to reinstate his spiritual endeavor through worship of God.

Christian Science demonstration displaces the mortal concept while caring for the human being. And Christian Science has the authority and power to bring about that displacement in every case. In *Rudimental Divine Science* Mrs. Eddy writes, "Christian Science erases from the minds of invalids their mistaken belief that they live in or because of matter, or that a so-called material organism controls the health or existence of mankind, and induces rest in God, divine Love, as caring for all the conditions requisite for the well-being of man" (p. 12). What truly facilitates this healing action is correct and successful practice in care.

Spiritual healing and restoration is a divine provision that cannot be frustrated by the human condition or by mortal claims. Physical symptoms are subdued and yield through the God-inspired expression of our true, spiritual nature.

In a situation where extended care is needed, it does not necessarily follow that such care is supporting an unprogressive experience. Only the mortal misconception of life claims that certain circumstances are nothing more than a perpetual care situation or that nursing aid is not sufficiently spiritual to support progress and healing. Until the human family advances beyond extensive care situations, we will need to master them. Each stage of the human situation must be brought under divine authority.

When someone we know has a challenge to overcome, the atmosphere surrounding that individual ought to be scientific: only pure, vigorous, spiritual witnessing should be admitted. This is far more helpful than our wondering how someone is getting along, or perhaps even speculating over what kind of ailment he has or how old he is. The pure atmosphere of exact, scientific thinking upholds our theological convictions, and this is the care we owe each other.

Our thoughts in the presence of the sick register our own spiritual strength or weakness. They contribute to our consistent progress or lack of it, and measure to what degree we are nurturing a sense of God's idea, man, or are caretakers for the mortal concept. The aim of dedicated care is a progressive mastery of mortality for all mankind.

It is not unusual for those engaged in Christian Science practice and nursing care to deal with the deeper challenges of human experience. These are the very occasions when they can help most effectually to meet the need through demonstrated spiritual strength. But human instinct would suggest that it is conveniently possible to avoid contact with these deeper challenges. This argument would also suggest that Christian Science nursing and practitioner work are unattractive fields of endeavor.

Staying away from the deep demands or being satisfied with the ordinary preoccupations of materialism may leave us metaphysically undeveloped and could seem to confer mysterious power on human difficulties. Willingness to participate in meeting the deep demands seasons our understanding with experience and develops our spiritual capacities. We become inspired to help others through difficult human situations because we have the assurance of the total unreality of evil and the conviction that healing is inevitable.

The greatest awareness of true power possible in human life comes through spiritual demonstration and healing. Such experiences teach us that sickness and death are empty threats. They are not awful possibilities that are able to violate our theology. The reward we receive for helping others or for facing these challenges ourselves and demonstrating our theology every step of the way is great spiritual advancement. Through such growth there will be more among us who find the way opening for a career as a Christian Science practitioner or nurse. This kind of dedication to further spiritual attainments must take form in order for us to advance the Cause of Christian Science.

The existence of Christian Science nursing services and facilities does not guarantee the fulfillment of their spiritual purpose. That guarantee is forged through the lives of individual Christian Scientists engaged in the dedicated practice of their theology. The experience and spiritual understanding of the Christian Science nurses and practitioners, of the patients, and of the entire staff, form the actual structure of a nursing facility. This is the "steel" that is immovable in the storm. It supports each one and all together in the progressive demonstration of the immortality of man.

There is much to be done in the line of spiritual development if we are to achieve greater measures of Christian healing for mankind. It can be done, and it will be. It *must* be, in the fulfillment of divine requirements. Every student who maintains a progressive, daily practice of Christian Science is helping to prepare the climate of thought that brings increased healing. Human consciousness needs to expect more, and be inspired in pursuing more.

Human welfare is both an individual and a collective demonstration. It involves our relationships with each other but actually rests on the individual's relationship to God. Love for God is what impels us to develop our spiritual capacities in Christ-healing. Through this development, the love we feel toward our fellowman, with its deep yearning to help lift the scourge of disease and death from the human family, will be manifest in ever-increasing proofs of divine Science.

—*Geraldine Schiering*

TIMELESS HEALING

If you need healing, please don't take time to read this editorial! Take just a moment of eternity.

Timeless healing sounds a little like the description of a cure that has stood the test of time. Yes, those who look to God for blessing could easily identify prayer as an ageless way to find answers to the pressing problems of mortality. But we can probe even more deeply to uncover the timeless nature of divine healing. Then prayer will become increasingly effective. In fact, we will heal as Jesus did, and as he wanted us to do.

Christ-healing is timeless healing because it is free of time. The Bible hints at timelessness: "Jesus Christ the same yesterday, and to-day, and for ever" (Heb. 13:8). From earliest Biblical days, the healing touch of the Christ has been felt. Even today, it's still a tender presence, uplifting and blessing. If you want to feel this gentle power, acknowledge it as ever-present in your consciousness "yesterday, and to-day, and for ever."

Imagine what it means to be free of time. Catch just a glimpse of this freedom and you will find true healing. Mary Baker Eddy used a number of words and phrases to throw fresh light on the nature of time (see *Science and Health with Key to the Scriptures*, p. 595). Here are two of them: (1) mortal measurements; (2) matter. Most people think of healing in the context of time. That is, it takes time for problems to develop (even difficulties that arrive suddenly take at least a moment). And it takes time to care for them. But timeless healing involves the forsaking of time. A "fasting" from mortal measurements, a denial of matter. Jesus healed because he was so filled with love, so endowed with the Christ. He didn't measure people with mortality. He didn't characterize them as objects of matter. His measure of an individual was Christliness, the eternal nature God has instilled within each of us.

Take a simple example of how differently most of the world approaches healing. Suppose some kind of discord develops. Perhaps a physical problem. The world's way of dealing with such human flaws involves time. And what does that mean? Moments, even hours, of dwelling on matter—measuring and emphasizing it. Typically people assess their level of discomfort—light or severe. Maybe they measure temperature, a heartbeat, blood pressure, how long they've endured the condition. Mortal measurements are an affirmation of matter. Classifying it, observing it, and often fearing it. The human mind says of this so-called substance, "I can measure you. You define me. You are my reality. You are rooted in the reality of time." But the Science of Christianity lifts us radically out of the quagmire of measuring matter to see ourselves as spiritual and Christly, the same "yesterday, and to-day, and for ever." Timeless.

The Christ is an eternal, elevating impulsion in consciousness. This compassionate presence would have us affirm Spirit. It reveals Spirit as immeasurable, unconfined, infinite. When we prayerfully acknowledge, with love and conviction, that boundless Spirit is our true substance, mortal limitations and inharmonies diminish. Sometimes quickly. Healing through Spirit leads us to yearn not so much for freedom *in* matter, as freedom *from* matter. Time-based healing would have us emphasize getting better from here on forward. Timeless healing would include getting better from here on back! That's right, real freedom doesn't happen if we simply think of our existence as on a timeline where discord has a beginning point and prayer is based on persuading God to get us out of trouble by tomorrow. We are liberated when we begin waking to realize that we aren't on a timeline at all. We've never been in matter. We can't and won't allow ourselves to be measured as if we are a condition of mortality. We are Christly. Real identity is right here in eternity, in Spirit's timeless allness.

Eternity is not something that happens in the future. It isn't endless time. Instead of the lengthening of time, it is the elimination of time. As Mrs. Eddy so deftly put it, ". . . time is no part of eternity" (*Science and Health*, p. 468). Her challenge to time has, to me, a ring of what St. John the Revelator described—an angel showing that as we see all creation coming from Spirit, we'll demonstrate "that there should be time no longer" (Rev. 10:6). There will be no delay in our life to expressing God's perfection.

Once I had a hacking cough that persisted for a long time—at least that's the mortal measurement I assigned the condition. I just couldn't seem to shake it. Then one day while I was praying about the unreality of time, I felt a sense of freedom from mortality, a kind of immortality, or heaven. It was as though the nurturing influence of the Christ liberated me from the confines of time as I pondered the powerlessness of "mortal measurements" and "matter." The cough suddenly stopped. I believe time stopped. I glimpsed and felt a sense of eternity. In that moment, God became more real to me than the cough. A spiritual view of reality overtook mortality. I could cough in time, but not in eternity!

A time-based approach to healing struggles within matter. Matter is the human mind's self-limiting measurements. It is an outline of life's restrictions. Timeless healing, on the other hand, relinquishes matter. It yields to real being as the unbounded, unrestricted, unlimited expression of Spirit. When we love God as our reality, a measure of Christliness emerges in our consciousness and is portrayed in our life as a sense of well-being, a feeling of joy and inner peace, a conviction of our true innocence and purity. We don't lose our substance, but we begin living it on a permanent basis.

When you treat a situation or condition through prayer, think of timeless healing. You're not stuck in matter or mortality, always trying to measure it and enhance it. You are expressive of Spirit's endless harmony because you are forever cherished as God's flawless child. You simply have no time in your life for anything but eternity!

—*Nathan A. Talbot*

To Avoid Doing It Wrongly, Do It Rightly

*M*any commands and useful directives are warnings of what not to do: Don't drive through a red light; Don't put your hand on a hot stove; "Say *No* to drugs," and so on. In the *Manual of The Mother Church*, Mary Baker Eddy gives "A Rule for Motives and Acts," and its last sentence is a warning against doing a lot of things wrongly. It reads, "The members of this Church should daily watch and pray to be delivered from all evil, from prophesying, judging, condemning, counseling, influencing or being influenced erroneously" (*Manual*, Art. VIII, Sect. 1).

These words had long been familiar to me. I knew them by heart. Wanting to be obedient, I went over them frequently, if not daily. One day, though, I realized how far my practice fell short of real obedience. Not only did I review this rule less than daily, but my obedience to it was less than real doing. After all, one could read a recipe all day, know it by heart, repeat it over and over, but that would never make or bake the cake. The instructions must be carried out or there's no end product.

Then, how could I do a better job of actually watching and praying to be delivered from doing all those things erroneously? As I listened to divine Mind for an answer, it soon occurred to me that when I was a child learning arithmetic, I wanted to be delivered from adding and subtracting, multiplying and dividing, erroneously. And how did I achieve that? By constantly practicing the right method. And the more adept I became at adding and multiplying rightly, the more thoroughly I was delivered from performing these functions wrongly.

That seemed logical. Perhaps, then, there was a right way to prophesy, judge, condemn, counsel, influence and be influenced. So I searched Concordances to the Bible and to Mrs. Eddy's writings and found that there are indeed right ways of doing all these things, as well as warnings against doing them wrongly.

Special insight, with practical results, came from the study of *prophesying*, and I'll expand on that shortly. But first, let's consider *judging*. Christ Jesus gives a vital directive in a single sentence: "Judge not according to the appearance, but judge righteous judgment" (John 7:24). Don't judge according to outward appearances, he warns us. That, surely, would be judging erroneously. But how often we tend to do this without realizing how deceptive appearances are! The physical senses, which have no intelligence or knowledge of God's perfect creation, cannot tell us what's actually true of anyone or anything. So judging on that basis is false judgment.

To "judge righteous judgment" we need to plunge beneath surface appearances. This demands the spiritual assessment that asks: "What is spiritually true of this situation? What does God know of it? How does He judge it?" Being watchful to judge from this standpoint, keeping our thought on the absolute spiritual reality of perfect God and His unflawed, spiritual creation, we're delivered from the constant temptation to judge erroneously.

Condemning was an interesting one. It seemed so negative that I expected to find only warnings against it. But no. My research revealed Jesus' strong condemnation of hypocrisy, materialism, sin of all kinds. And *Science and Health* by Mrs. Eddy warned that if we fail to condemn evil we're actually nurturing it (see 448:5–7). To avoid nurturing evil, then, we *must* condemn it—not as a fact but as a falsity. This is condemning rightly.

The wrong condemning we need to be delivered from is condemning persons. Jesus' example is so clear. He didn't condemn a diseased or insane or sinful person. He condemned the disease, the insanity, the sin, rebuking the devil, or evil, while healing and restoring the individual. When we're alert to condemn evil in the most thorough way possible—by affirming with conviction its powerlessness, unreality, utter nothingness, and its separateness from the true nature of anyone or anything—we're delivered from condemning persons and thus condemning erroneously.

Counseling. Today's society is filled with counselors—psychological, academic, marriage, financial, career, legal, and so on. People are used to getting lots of human advice. Some of this may be helpful, some not. How can we tell? And if someone asks *us* for advice, how do we know if we're counseling rightly or wrongly?

One way is to check to see if we're giving merely a human opinion. *Science and Health* has a good deal to say about personal opinions, and there's not much favorable comment! Perhaps such opinions would fit what the Psalmist calls "the devices of the people." "The Lord bringeth the counsel of the heathen to nought: he maketh the devices of the people of none effect. The counsel of the Lord standeth for ever, the thoughts of his heart to all generations" (Ps. 33:10, 11).

"The counsel of the Lord" is the only absolutely trustworthy counsel. And we can be sure we're counseling rightly when we turn someone to God and point out His laws and the rewards of obeying them; when we give assurance of the one supreme Mind always guiding its own ideas unerringly and of the individual's God-given ability to hear and respond to this guidance. When we counsel in this way, we're delivered from the temptation to push our personal opinions and thus counsel erroneously.

Influencing. If the world is full of counselors, it's even more full of influences. And these are more subtle. They're often mental and unseen. We may not always realize our influence upon others. Even if it's quite unintentional, it's still an influence. And if it's a wrong one—matter-based or sense-oriented, self-willed or opinionated—it's to be avoided. The remedy is to be sure we're influencing rightly by doing good, actually embodying good by living more consistently as the very evidence of God. As *Science and Health* puts it: "Your influence for good depends upon the weight you throw into the right scale. The good you do and embody gives you the only power obtainable" (p. 192).

And what about *being influenced?* Being ignorant of or apathetic about the subtle or aggressive suggestions permeating the atmosphere of human thought is allowing ourselves to be influenced erroneously. The *Church Manual* includes a daily duty to defend oneself against "aggressive mental suggestion" (see *Manual*, Art. VIII, Sect. 6). One way of doing this is to acknowledge no other mind but the one infinite Mind, God; to realize that because there's only one Mind, there's actually no aggressive mortal mind to suggest or to malpractice, nor is there a susceptible mortal mind to be influenced by such suggestion or malpractice.

As we recognize that the only influence we can really be under is the Christ, the divine influence always present in every human consciousness everywhere; as we accept that Christ is the divine message from God always telling us what's true about ourselves and everyone else, we're delivered from being influenced erroneously.

Now back to *prophesying.* To fear the future, to expect some harmful outcome, to brood over *what ifs?*, to predict any development of evil, would be to prophesy erroneously.

And the remedy? Be a true prophet. In this regard the Glossary of *Science and Health* provides a couple of illuminating spiritual definitions: "Elias. Prophecy; spiritual evidence opposed to material sense; Christian Science, with which can be discerned the spiritual fact of whatever the material senses behold; . . . " and "Prophet. A spiritual seer; disappearance of material sense before the conscious facts of spiritual Truth" (pp. 585, 593).

A prophet sees spiritually. With the lens of Christian Science, he sees through material appearances and beholds spiritual facts. So doing, he witnesses the progressive disappearance of the material sense of things as he becomes more and more conscious of what is divinely true. And thus he's being delivered from prophesying falsely and from its consequences.

I felt uplifted and enlightened by this research and the insight that had prompted it. It gave me a way of more fully obeying the admonition in "A Rule for Motives and Acts." And that Rule has glowed with a new light for me ever since.

A week or two after my study I found myself suddenly besieged with all the symptoms of a very heavy cold or influenza. "Oh no, not again!" I reacted, as the prospect of an all-too-familiar pattern of suffering flooded my thinking. But immediately came the realization that this was prophesying erroneously—predicting the development of evil. And the remedy? Be a true prophet. Be a real, spiritual seer. Hold consciously to the "facts of spiritual Truth" until I witness the disappearance of this painful, disruptive, material sense of my being.

Immediately I started claiming spiritual facts— like my eternal relation to my Father-Mother God as His likeness, therefore spiritual, not material. As such I was unavailable to any influence from popular beliefs in contagion or susceptibility to weather conditions, from medical concepts about patterns of development and duration of diseases, and so on. The only influence I could really be subject to was the Christ, the divine presence always speaking to my consciousness, telling me of my unassailable perfection as God's image, of my harmony, my health, my wholeness, right here, right now; telling me that these facts are the truth for everyone, everywhere.

I don't remember the exact reasoning that came to me, but it was along these lines, and it was expressed in vigorous affirmations of truth and denials of error. I wasn't about to put up with error's imposition. I persisted in this prayer for a few minutes. I was becoming more of a true prophet, more of a spiritual seer.

In not much longer than it has taken you to read these lines I felt the symptoms receding until I was completely free, and I remained so. That false, material sense of me had disappeared "before the conscious facts of spiritual Truth." By being something of a true prophet, I'd been delivered from prophesying the development of a pattern of suffering and from the consequences of such false prophecy. It's a healing I've always remembered with great gratitude for the Rules Mrs. Eddy has given in the *Manual*.

Everyone has the right and privilege to be a true prophet, a righteous judge, an alert condemner of evil, a spiritual counselor, a purifying influence. And then he'll find himself under no lesser influence than the Christ. And he'll be obeying "A Rule for Motives and Acts" in a meaningful, practical way—a way that heals.

—*David C. Driver*

TRUTH HANDLES CRIME

*C*hristian Science teaches that there is one Mind, infinite good, and that there is no power apart from this Mind. It also teaches that man, whether spoken of individually or collectively, is the reflection of this Mind. It declares that this Mind alone made the universe and controls it. Christian Science also uncovers the false beliefs of human thought as errors which are exposed and ended by Truth. It tells the truth about error, and demonstrates its nothingness as a suppositional power opposed to God. In doing this Christian Science follows the teaching of Jesus, enabling his followers to understand his sayings, repeat his mighty works, and attain to his resurrection.

Mrs. Eddy has written that if we would scientifically prove evil's unreality we must first see sin's claim and then annihilate it. In pondering this important matter let us turn to the words of Jesus, who was never the victim of evil, but who overcame error in all its forms. In the eighth and tenth chapters of John, Jesus refers to evil as a liar, a thief, and a murderer. These terms brand it as criminal. In *Science and Health,* on page 105, our Leader states that mortal mind "is the criminal in every case."

Phases of belief which seem to be included in the term "criminality" are plotting, unfolding the evil plan, and escape from justice while pinning the crime upon the innocent. Error from the beginning has asserted its innocence and has tried to fasten upon God the aspect of the liar and the murderer. But there is no escape for error from divine justice, because the mark of the beast is upon its forehead. This mark cannot be erased or transferred to divinity. The sinner is mortal mind, and we cannot remove God's waymarks.

The terms "invasion" and "trespass" are also associated with the word "crime." Trespass implies the encroaching upon "another's presence, privileges, rights or the like," while invasion may be defined as "entering with an armed force with hostile intent." Do not these definitions apply to sin and disease in all their forms?

Any attempted invasion of one's consciousness by fear, sin, discouragement, or other evil belief is a crime of mental trespass. This is prevented by knowing that real consciousness dwells with the divine Mind, where error never enters. The constant activity of good in consciousness leaves no opportunity for error to abide there. As the nothingness of the carnal mind is clearly discerned, its claims of aggressive mental suggestion and malicious animal magnetism are proved powerless. This is actually occurring in the experience of everyone who is honestly applying the teachings of Christian Science in his daily life.

It may be said that all error's claims to power come under the head of crime. In every case the crime is the denial of Spirit's allness, and the suffering this brings to anyone who entertains the lie. No community is safe which harbors a criminal. Would we shield a murderer in our home? Then, how much more should we deny room in our consciousness to an aggressive, destructive thought!

Our Leader warns us to be as watchful against entertaining false beliefs as we would be in guarding against the approach of murderers and thieves (see *Science and Health*, p. 234). When the right thinker and doer is troubled in thought or body, let him awake to handle error as claiming to be present in the preliminary stages of crime, and know that the omnipresence and omniaction of divine law never allow error in any form to exist or to enter the domain of infinity, which belongs to God.

One sometimes hears the remark, "What a crime!" when reference is being made to a lovely character bound by a so-called incurable disease. That is just what it is—a crime, in which the innocent one is made to suffer and the perpetrator goes free. If the case were handled from this angle, the carnal mind would be arrested and delivered to divine justice, the crime stopped, and the sufferer liberated. Disease, sin, poverty, old age, and death are the crimes of mortal mind. Every claim of life, substance, and intelligence in matter is a sin against God and humanity. They can be permanently disposed of only by the operation of divine law in human consciousness.

All the endeavor of the ages to stamp out crime by punishing and destroying people, has not ended wrongdoing. Is it not reasonable, then, to suppose that something else is the criminal, that something else is the liar, the thief, adulterer, or murderer? How is it that Christian justice has so missed the paramount statement of Jesus that mortal mind, "the strong man," is what must be bound? (see Matt. 12:29, Mark 3:27.) Since mortal mind is the wrongdoer, false beliefs are always the means through which the sin is perpetrated. Then let us dispose of false beliefs rather than condemn persons or groups of persons.

As we understand these things clearly, we cease to regard each other as enemies. We no longer think that we must get rid of individuals or groups who seem to menace harmony. We refrain from fearing our neighbors and do not appear dangerous to them. It will become increasingly plain to all men that the only aggressor there is, is mortal mind, and that it is an illusion. Then its suppositional acts of trespass, invasion, deceit, and destruction will no more have power to harm us, and will cease to seem to occur. So error will finally go to its native nothingness as humanity yields to the reign of Truth.

Because evil is unreal, it has no power or presence, no agent through which to enter our experience or rob us of aught that has come to us through obedience to God. It has no power to trespass upon our right of continuous demonstration of good, drive us out of our position of constant spiritual unfoldment, or take possession of aught that rightfully serves us or belongs to us. Let us often remember that our spiritual understanding, our ability to use it, and the divine results which come from it are "in the secret place of the most High," safe "under the shadow of the Almighty," and will endure beyond the end of all error and throughout eternity (see Ps. 91:1). That which is criminal is temporal. That which is spiritual is indestructible. Therefore the human journey which is allied with spiritual understanding is safe, unobstructed, steadfast, progressive, victorious.

The reason why crime seems so prevalent today may be that Christian Science is uncovering as criminal the elemental nature of so-called mortal mind. Our Leader writes in *Science and Health* (p. 102) that "the looms of crime" in mortal thought are weaving "more complicated and subtle" webs of error in these latter days; but these are merely the gossamer webs of illusion, without power to catch, or hold, or bind that thought which is alert to the nothingness of material sense and equipped with spiritual understanding. Mrs. Eddy says that Truth will sweep away "the gossamer web of mortal illusion" (*Science and Health*, p. 403). A "gossamer web" is frailty itself. It is no part of that upon which it rests. It is attached only by the slenderest threads, which the wind easily breaks; and the web floats away, never to return. The action of God's law breaks the threads of false belief and error vanishes.

As Christian Science uncovers error, it always shows it to be unreal, and therefore leaves no fear of it. Until every phase of error is uncovered by Truth it retains the appearance of reality. It is well to have evil's claim of awfulness fully exposed, because then its lie is silenced by the understanding of one Mind, God, even infinite good. Divine Love accomplishes this uncovering only as human thought knows enough of Truth to discern error's unreality and to prove it. Love equips the individual who is reaching out to God, with sufficient spiritual understanding to demonstrate the nothingness of uncovered false belief.

Here let us recall the illustration of Christian Science practice which Mrs. Eddy gives, beginning on page 430 of *Science and Health*, and which is referred to in the marginal note of the first paragraph as "A mental court case." It is a case of crime, of "foul conspiracy" against "Mortal Man," which Christian Science uncovers and handles. In the first part of the case innocent "Mortal Man" is arraigned before the "Court of Error." There is no defense there, and "Judge Medicine" pronounces the death sentence. Here Christian Science takes up the case and appeals to the "Court of Spirit." As the attorney for the victim and with the Bible as "the supreme statute-book," Christian Science bases its plea for reversal of the unjust sentence in the "Court of Error" upon the spiritual facts of man's relationship to God. Christian Science demands the arrest of "Personal Sense" on the criminal charges of "perjury, treason, and conspiracy against" man's "rights and life."

In this trial Christian Science detects, uncovers, and denounces the subtlety, falsity, injustice, and murderous intent of "Personal Sense." It repudiates sense-testimony, wins the reversal of the decree of the "Court of Error" and the recommendation from the Chief Justice that "Health-laws, Mesmerism, Hypnotism, Oriental Witchcraft, and Esoteric Magic be publicly executed." The case closes with the liberation of "Mortal Man" and the restoration to him of health and freedom. Justice is done, and all that seemed to have been taken from the innocent victim is restored to him. The plea of Christian Science has healed the sick at "the bar of Truth." This might be carefully considered in every case which comes to Christian Science for healing.

In Jesus' trial also, the criminality of the carnal mind is uncovered. Had Jesus treated the situation as a personal attack in which he must vindicate himself, this would not have been accomplished, and he would not have had the opportunity to prove evil powerless to harm him. He let it uncover itself in its elemental nature as suppositional enmity against good. Then he demonstrated that there is no such power or reality in the human or the divine experience.

From the beginning to the end of Jesus' career, the carnal mind appeared as the would-be destroyer of God's emissary. It was not Herod the Great, who reigned at Jesus' birth, or Herod Antipas, who was in Jerusalem at the time of Jesus' trial, or Pilate, or Caiaphas, or Judas who was the criminal. Neither was it the priests or the mob, for Jesus defended himself against none of these. He even called Judas "friend" (see Matt. 26:50). He let the full belief of mortal mind loose itself against him, in order that, being uncovered, it might be seen and destroyed. The angels who had charge over him during his earthly experience, did no harm to the men who came against him, but delivered Jesus from the thrusts of mortality and exposed the nothingness of evil's claim to invade his experience, alter his course, or destroy his identity. Jesus rose triumphant from the tomb, and later ascended into the fullness of infinite Life and Love.

It is essential for every Christian Scientist to bear these things clearly in mind; to remember that no man is his enemy, and that he is the enemy of no man; that his warfare is with false belief and not persons; that it is divine law which delivers him from evil; that his defense is of God; that he will outlive all of evil's attempts, and will see mortality yield to divinity; and that he too will behold the eternal reality of infinite good.

Every step of the way there are angels, divine intuitions, to guard and guide the true Christian Scientist. Sometimes they hide him where material sense cannot find him. Sometimes they accompany him when he stands face to face with evil suggestions, and bring him through the warfare unscathed. Again, they come to him in silent prayer and lift his eyes to see the hosts of heaven allied with him. And, finally, they open the tomb of material sense to set free the imprisoned thought and swing wide the gates of eternal harmony, wherein he may enter as the faithful follower of Truth.

The way of the Christian Scientist is not dangerous, but safe. He proves the powerlessness and unreality of evil at every point. He does not become the victim of mental crime, but demonstrates the falsity of criminality, crime, and criminal, in every experience. He discovers the presence of heaven everywhere, the allness of God, good. He is not weary on the journey, because he does not have to fight against an evil entity, but has only to know God, omnipotent good. And through all the journey he understands and loves the Way-shower and our Leader, for they have mapped out the straight and safe path, have shortened the way and illumined every bit of the road with divine light. There is nothing to hinder our rapid progress heavenward.

—*Julia M. Johnston*

AN UNAMBIGUOUS CHRISTIANITY

☙❧

The Apostle Paul was not a compromising man. When it came to the message and standards of Christ, he didn't retreat. He didn't revise his message to conciliate his audience. His strong words—and his tender words—were designed to revise his audience in order to bring their lives into harmony with Christ.

And it isn't as though Paul went untested! He nearly lost his life several times, and he was frequently harassed and persecuted by those who resisted and even hated what he had to say. But his faith and, in some ways more important, his love remained steadfast. He may have been resolute and unbending, but his life shone and radiated with love.

His message reached many hearts. And the life-giving power of God that changed the course of Paul's life changed the course of their lives as well. His Gentile converts were introduced to a new moral, ethical, and spiritual culture. As so much of this was at odds with the society that surrounded them, it was natural for them to meet together to support each other, to dig deeper into the realm and purpose of Spirit, and to celebrate their redemption from sin.

Today's world is vastly different technologically from Paul's, yet there are surprising correspondences in the mental forces that sway both societies. The paganism, superstition, fundamentalism, and hedonism of today are not so different from their first-century counterparts. Even a brief search of the Internet—our most modern venue of twenty-first-century communication—reveals how prevalent these old beliefs and practices are. Today, Christians still need to find their path through these icebergs that would capsize their faith.

Many people are lamenting the moral decline evident around the world and the price it exacts in wasted human lives. Legislators, social workers, educators, parents, church officials, are actively searching for answers. Some are posing this question: What is Christianity's response to moral decline? The more one studies the Bible and the writings of Mary Baker Eddy, the more one recognizes how appropriate this answer would be: What we need is an unambiguous Christianity.

What does this mean?

Paul gives us a clue in his letter to the Philippians: "For to me to live is Christ..." (Phil. 1:21). The English scholar J. B. Lightfoot interprets Paul's words in this way: "'*To me,*' whatever it may be to others: ... '*life is Christ.*' 'I live only to serve Him, only to commune with Him; I have no conception of life apart from Him.'" (*St. Paul's Epistle to the Philippians* [Peabody, Mass.: Hendrickson Publishers, 1987], p. 92) The question for the Christian today, as it was then, is, Can I sincerely repeat Paul's words?

This total dedication to Christ was notable not only among the early Christians but also among Mrs. Eddy's students as they worked to "reinstate primitive Christianity and its lost element of healing" (*Manual of The Mother Church*, p. 17). Christ Jesus taught his disciples: "Ye are the light of the world. A city that is set on an hill cannot be hid." (Matt. 5:14) His true followers did not turn to Christ, Truth, only when necessary. Christ was their life, defined their motives and purpose, animated them day by day; and the works of Christ, healing and redemption, shone in the world. These disciples bore witness to the fact that Christ Jesus laid down his human life so that God, divine Life itself, would be revealed to humanity. The Master's unparalleled sacrifice, his unambiguous love, moved them and transformed them. They simply couldn't help dedicating themselves to living lives of unselfed love.

Here is another insight into the nature of "unambiguous" Christianity. It's recorded by the Christian historian Eusebius. While visiting a church near Ephesus, the Apostle John met a youngster who he felt had particular promise, and so he requested one of the elders of the church to look closely after him. This was done for some time.

As the lad grew older, however, this care was relaxed. Then, Eusebius reports, the boy "was led sadly astray by others of his own age who were idle, dissolute, and evil-livers. First they led him on by expensive entertainments; then they took him with them when they went out at night to commit robbery; then they urged him to take part in even greater crimes. Little by little he fell into their ways; and like a hard-mouthed powerful horse he dashed off the straight road, and taking the bit between his teeth rushed down the precipice the more violently because of his immense vitality. Completely renouncing God's salvation, he was no longer content with petty offenses, but, as his life was already in ruins, he decided to commit a major crime and suffer the same fate as the others. He took these same young renegades and formed them into a gang of bandits of which his was the master mind, surpassing them all in violence, cruelty, and bloodthirstiness."

Around this time, John returned and asked after this young man, and he was told what had occurred. Greatly disturbed, he immediately went to him. Eusebius says, "When he arrived at the place, and was seized by the bandits' sentry-group, he made no attempt to escape and asked no mercy, but shouted: 'This is what I have come for: take me to your leader.' . . . as John approached, he [the young man] recognized him, and filled with shame, turned to flee. But John ran after him as hard as he could, forgetting his years and calling out: 'Why do you run away from me, child . . . ? You still have hopes of life. I will account to Christ for you. If need be, I will gladly suffer your death, as the Lord suffered death for us; to save you I will give my own life. Stop! believe! Christ sent me.'

"When he heard this, the young man stopped and stood with his eyes on the ground; then he threw down his weapons; then he trembled and began to weep bitterly. . . . Then he [John] brought him back to the church, interceded for him with many prayers, shared with him the ordeal of continuous fasting, . . . and did not leave him, we are told, till he had restored him to the Church, giving a perfect example of true repentance and a perfect proof of regeneration, the trophy of a visible resurrection." (*The History of the Church from Christ to Constantine* [Hammondsworth, England: Dorset Press, 1984], pp. 129–131.)

John had heard Jesus' parable of the lost sheep (see Luke 15:3–7). If one sheep among one hundred was lost, wouldn't the shepherd go after that one until it was found? The world needs more of these shepherds, more Christians who are willing to give all in love for another. Many ask, Where's the time? What about my other obligations? How could I produce the effect John did? And these questions are not presented lightly. But we are faced with the fact that John had nothing more pressing, nothing more urgent to do, than to fulfill the two commandments on which "hang all the law and the prophets" (see Matt. 22:35–40): to love God with all his heart and all his soul and all his mind and to love his neighbor as himself. "All" evidently meant exactly that to him. And he apparently knew God was equal to the need.

Some people try to cushion the moral and spiritual demands of Christianity—afraid, perhaps, that they will drive people away or expose their own discomfort with the standards of Christian life. There is no such fuzziness in the Christian Science textbook, *Science and Health with Key to the Scriptures*. For example, Mrs. Eddy writes, "The commandment, 'Thou shalt not commit adultery,' is no less imperative than the one, 'Thou shalt not kill'" (*Science and Health*, p. 56). Later in this same book she writes: "Honesty is spiritual power. Dishonesty is human weakness, which forfeits divine help" (p. 453). There is no ambiguity here. True Christianity stands over this age like the polestar, providing the spiritual guidance needed to avoid the misery that comes from sin—the guidance that enables so many to find their way back to health and goodness. How could we make this trip if we were never quite sure where our guiding star was?

Moral discipline is a manifestation of divine Love. The Ten Commandments, the Sermon on the Mount, and the teachings of Christian Science, which embrace this Biblical instruction, reveal the love of God. Mankind needs this unambiguous guidance. Jesus' resurrection reveals the moral and spiritual power of that guidance; and today, faithful practice of the Bible's precepts, together with an understanding of the divine law that underlies them, continues to resurrect life from sin and the suffering it brings. As we come to recognize Love's purpose revealed through moral law, we will readily acknowledge the unchanging standards of Christian life. This will not make us rigid or condemnatory or holier-than-thou. We will simply be reflecting more of the healing and resurrecting power of Christ, Truth. We'll be expressing the love that spares mankind much suffering.

How do we get to this point? Has the meaning of Jesus' life really touched our hearts? Has it come alive in us? Is it baptizing us and awakening us to life in and of God? Have the potency and purpose of divine Love, made evident through the revelation of Christian Science to this age, begun to take hold of us? Are they doing so with sufficient force that we are willing to lay down all for Christ, to begin a new life with Christ at its helm? Here we begin to see the nature of the battle Christianity inaugurates. It's between our own sense of life and the life that Christ leads us to. When we're ready to give up a material sense of selfhood, with its wants and aims and sense of right, and yield to the reality of man's being in Spirit, our spiritual transformation begins.

Mrs. Eddy writes, "Self-renunciation of all that constitutes a so-called material man, and the acknowledgment and achievement of his spiritual identity as the child of God, is Science that opens the very flood-gates of heaven; whence good flows into every avenue of being, cleansing mortals of all uncleanness, destroying all suffering, and demonstrating the true image and likeness" (*Miscellaneous Writings*, p. 185). As this takes place, Christians find that they have the moral and spiritual stature needed to heal and redeem mankind.

In the light of this, has it struck you that today's cultural emphasis on self-fulfillment is actually anti-Christian? The intense focus on self-fulfillment is one of the unsavory products of materialism and it weakens people's moral sense. The cultivation and admiration of unselfishness are sacrificed. In this atmosphere, career comes before family, closing the deal comes before ethics, doing things "my way" comes before cooperation or concern about others, sexual indulgence comes before morality, and condemnation comes instead of healing and reform. Thus the Christian is faced with such questions as, When I put my personal needs and desires, my development, my self-actualization, my will, above all else, how do I fulfill the two commandments cited by Jesus? Could I be as successful as John in rescuing another from sin?

In *Science and Health* and in her other writings, Mrs. Eddy notes the moral values that are requisite for progress and the practice of Christian healing. She writes of the Christian virtues of self-immolation, self-abnegation, self-sacrifice, self-forgetfulness, self-consecration, self-denial. She also exposes the sinful tendency of self-satisfaction, self-love, self-will, self-seeking, self-aggrandizement, and self-justification. In many ways, these latter terms show how far segments of society have wandered from embracing the essential character of Christian life.

It is the consciousness and experience of God's divine power and love that equips one to pursue a different life, a truly fulfilling life. A man healed by Jesus of blindness declared, "One thing I know, that, whereas I was blind, now I see" (John 9:25). The Christian reaffirms his words, having gained a new vision of being, a vision of what Jesus' life is continuing to tell mankind about life—about God, His children, His will. The Christian's prayer changes from pleading and hoping to affirming—affirming that God, Spirit, alone is Life, the only creator, supreme Love, and that man is His spiritual, eternal likeness. Divine Love is reflected in the Christian's innermost being

and expressed in every thought and deed. This divine animus is greatly needed today.

Some will say: "But I don't feel this. How I wish I did, but I don't." Don't despair. If you desire to attain this, you surely will. We can begin by renouncing the claims materiality makes on our time and thoughts. We'll begin to carve out more and more occasions to submerge ourselves in Spirit, to feel deeply through prayer the infiniteness of Spirit and man's native purity as Spirit's image. If, like Naaman (see II Kings 5:1–15), we need to wash ourselves seven times in the river, or consciousness, of Life, we will. We may even do so seventy times a day. Purity is key to growth. Moral purity. A pure love. A pure devotion to goodness, unselfishness, honesty, spirituality. This is not beyond any one of us, because purity characterizes our true being.

Selfishness buries one in matter and so-called material comfort. Here or hereafter, this is a tomb we'll need to leave. Had John planned to spend days working with that young man? Yet he left all for Christ. Other considerations were put aside as Love led him to do everything he could to save one lost sheep. He was willing to lay down his own life in love for another.

Had Paul planned to spend three years in the desert communing with God as he made his way up the road to Damascus? We know he hadn't. Yet the glory of God that at first blinded him became the leading light of his life. He stayed faithful to that light.

The longer the disciples were with Jesus, the more most of them grew in moral strength. The more we imbibe the spirit of Christ revealed through the Bible and *Science and Health*, the more we grow in moral strength. Our lives become purer. They burn with a purer flame of Truth. The unselfish affections bloom, and the fruit is a greater ability to heal and to raise those dead in sin. Divine Love is not "self" conscious. The heart that is at one with Love beats strongly for mankind. As Jesus beheld the multitudes, he had compassion upon them.

Unambiguous Christianity stands firmly for the worship of Spirit alone in thought and life. It stands for total dedication to beholding man as God created him, in all his purity and glory—and for daily faithfulness to this ideal. It stands for loving one's neighbor as oneself. This is the moral force Christian Science brings into the world today.

—Richard C. Bergenheim

VIRGIN BIRTH: BEYOND HISTORY, A LIVING SPIRITUAL IDEA

When a new spiritual idea is borne to earth, the prophetic Scripture of Isaiah is renewedly fulfilled: "Unto us a child is born, . . . and his name shall be called Wonderful."

Science and Health *by Mary Baker Eddy, p. 109*

There is scarcely a more precious, sacred event in Christian history than the virgin birth of Christ Jesus. Nothing can deprive this event of its uniqueness, its foundational position in Christian theology, or its special significance to the Christian.

But the theology of Christian Science shows the timeless import of this historic event and explains that the virgin birth was not a miracle, not a departure from natural law, but a proof of the Science of real creation, in which God, Spirit, is the sole origin and continuity of man and the universe. "Those instructed in Christian Science," explains its Discoverer, Mrs. Eddy, "have reached the glorious perception that God is the only author of man. The Virgin-mother conceived this idea of God, and gave to her ideal the name of Jesus—that is, Joshua, or Saviour" (*Science and Health*, p. 29).

This is not to suggest that Christian Scientists expect physical generation to be repeated in this way. Quite the contrary. One of Mrs. Eddy's biographers writes, "Although the historic virgin birth played a key role in Mrs. Eddy's theology, she saw it as a unique event related to the uniqueness of Jesus' mission" (Robert Peel, *Mary Baker Eddy: The Years of Authority* [New York: Holt, Rinehart and Winston, 1977], p. 423). But while this unique proof of man's eternal unity with God can be indisputably located in a framework of time, the *laws* involved in the Science of creation transcend time. And among their offspring in this age are the practical demonstrations of Christian healing that are born of scientific prayer.

In fact, humanity is, to a degree, agreeing with the law of spiritual creation when it embraces the concept of prayer. Prayer signifies a willingness to turn from human causation to God. It acknowledges man's unity with God and concedes the possibility of divine impartation reaching human consciousness. Any "new spiritual idea" born of such communion can be said to be original, in a sense a "virgin birth."

But limited concessions to spiritual origin aren't enough. If humanity is to feel the constancy of divine relatedness that brings a full salvation from evil, then spiritual causation, the only truth of creation and the starting point of all real thought and action, cannot be perceived of as merely something that coexists with a real physical universe. The realization that religious orthodoxy is not in the least uncomfortable with the basic idea of divine intervention—*occasional* unity with God—should awaken Christian Scientists to ask why. And then to rise to the holy heights of the significance of virgin birth.

After all, the scribes and Pharisees of Jesus' day didn't question proof after Biblical proof of dependence on spiritual power to, by all appearances, aid men in what seemed their own power to create and to perpetuate life. They agreed that God enabled Sarah and Abraham to bear Isaac in old age; that God opened the wombs of Rachel and Hannah. But this same thought loathed the idea of pure divine sonship and crucified the man who embodied and taught it. Why?

Perhaps it had something to do with a basic misinterpretation. By misinterpreting Old Testament events and healings (and the healings of Jesus) to mean that God intervenes to adjust, multiply, and heal matter, the carnal mind could get away with believing that matter and Spirit were both real and could combine. It is above all the advent, life, and teachings of the sinless Jesus, illumined by Christian Science, that force mortal thought to face the correct interpretation of miracles and healings; to recognize them as proof of the utter nothingness of material life and intelligence. "This thought of human, material nothingness, which Science inculcates, enrages the carnal mind and is the main cause of the carnal mind's antagonism," Mrs. Eddy explains (*Science and Health*, p. 345).

Over the centuries, the carnal mind has found endless ways to avoid the fact of its own nothingness. It eventually found a way to adjust Christian theology to the virgin birth of Jesus by emphasizing its unique historical nature, rather than its timeless spiritual message. True, Jesus was God's "only begotten Son," but he was also the supreme earthly example of the truth that, spiritually, every one of us is right now God's son, Love's innocent offspring.

In recent times some theologians have called into question the factuality of the virgin birth itself. But nothing can forever hide the fact that the virgin birth did occur and pointed to the end of all compromise with the belief of intelligent matter. The living law of spiritual creation illustrated by the virgin birth is the basis of the inescapable demand on each of us to stop conforming to the world and be "born again." It is also the key to penetrating deeply the problem of evil and conflict and bringing salvation to mankind.

Virgin birth and individual salvation

The virgin birth gives definitive evidence that the doctrine of original sin is false, when this birth is understood as an illustration of the sinless, original being of all creation. It demonstrates that every real individuality has only one antecedent: God, Spirit. It proves that every individuality imparted by the one Father-Mother is pure, neither formed nor touched by genetics, chance, or heredity; and that each Soul-bestowed consciousness—forever unconditioned by past experience—is uncontaminated and unhaunted by mistake, disobedience, guilt, or condemnation.

Because these spiritual facts of creation are the reality, mortality is understood to be illusion. The human demand, therefore, fulfilled by Love's pure Christ-power only, is to see through the carnal mind's imposed illusion that we are material entities separated from divine Love and discover our real being as God's likeness. We must be "born again."

And what can this new birth be but the fruit of the virgin birth of spiritual ideas—ideas conceived and born of Spirit—that gradually but totally redeem human consciousness from error?

Perhaps the fundamental idea of Christian regeneration is clear to us, but the real problem is how to get from self-centered will and sensuality to the wholly spiritual power that transforms human life, heals us, and ultimately lifts us out of mortality. How do we approach the Science of creation that brought Jesus forth and that brings forth every idea that redeems and heals?

The fact is that as we become willing to exchange the belief in a self-justifying personal ego for the true conception of man as Love's idea, this Science approaches *us*. And the sacred task of both men and women is to yield to this dawning Christ-power that uplifts spiritual selfhood, especially spiritual womanhood, and prepares us to submit to the overshadowing love and creative power of the Holy Ghost. "The Holy Ghost shall come upon thee," the angel Gabriel explained to Mary, "and the power of the Highest shall overshadow thee." To which Mary responded, in moving, simple words whose outcome shook the whole foundation of genetic and atomic theory, "Behold the handmaid of the Lord; be it unto me according to thy word" (Luke 1:35, 38).

In Mary's example of uplifted womanhood we begin to understand the qualities of thought and character able to receive the conception of man as the idea of Love. Absolute faith and trust in God, remarkable courage, childlike expectancy of good, selfless obedience, purity of heart, meekness, unresistant receptivity—Mary's consciousness at that moment was the very embodiment of those Beatitudes that later open the Sermon on the Mount and would forever mark the way to overcome the world. Most certainly, this unworldliness—this humble sense of selfhood that knows it can do nothing without God—is, as always, "despised and rejected of men" (Isa. 53:3); but it is the only attitude that demonstrates unity with God and allows the Holy Ghost to penetrate human consciousness with the creative spiritual law that breaks through hereditary patterns of thought.

Since this uplifted consciousness is the "womb" where the infant idea of our original, sinless being is dawning, our necessity is to protect our new birth with purity of thought. Here is where the virgin birth of spiritual ideas in us begins its inevitable coincidence with the needs of mankind, with the universal body of human thought. We cannot surround the infant idea of our spiritual identity with mental purity without feeling the oneness and allness of the impartial love of God that embraces all simultaneously. Since, in truth, each of us fully individualizes the divine Mind, the substance of our own real identity consists of the pure consciousness of *all* of Mind's loved ideas. We falsely conceive our own substance and misunderstand the new birth when we fail to love another as ourselves.

At the same time, the uncompromising love needed to bear witness to heaven-born ideas teaches us the need to fast from the belief that evil has any actual presence or force with which to invade and divide real purity, the oneness of good. Our spiritual development is kept pure to the degree we reject the dualism that claims both good and evil to be real and to the degree we rid thought of ungodlike, unchristian thinking. Spirit, good, is infinite. In truth, there is neither opposition to this fact nor conflict within its allness.

Virgin birth and universal salvation

The virgin birth of Christ Jesus is certainly one of the most important, concrete proofs in history of the *oneness* of real being. It draws a clear line of distinction between what is true and what is not, between the unreality of matter and the reality of Spirit. It shows spiritual causation to be the foundation of mankind's salvation from all evil—from the entire mass of error coming from the belief that matter is the basis of life. This latter belief in multiple origins—in intelligent, living matter, or animal magnetism—would set up a creation in perpetual and inevitable conflict. Belief in more than the one Mind lays the groundwork for the ceaseless polarization of human thought and life. Male and female, science and art, science and religion, creativity and stability, gentleness and power, feeling and intellect, innocence and maturity, often seem to be in opposition to each other; and only the truth of matter's nothingness and Spirit's allness can resolve this conflict.

Mrs. Eddy writes: "One only of the following statements can be true: (1) that everything is matter; (2) that everything is Mind. Which one is it?" (*Science and Health*, p. 270). This uncompromising statement exposes the inconsistency of thinking we can continue to live with the occasional unity with God implied in divine intervention. We cannot, as Jesus warned, "serve God and mammon" (Matt. 6:24). The fact of being is that matter and Spirit (being opposites) cannot dwell together; *something must be all.* The carnal mind claims matter to be the nature and essence of all that is real. This claim is represented by various atheistic systems such as dialectical materialism and scientific materialism, and these thought systems prey, feed, and grow on conflict and separation. They embody the carnal mind's lust to cling to life in matter, its need to deny the divine idea of oneness, and its intent to swallow up everything that opposes it. Atheistic materialism represents total acceptance of material evidence. Its opposite, and its destroyer, cannot be, therefore, any system or theology that unscientifically mixes matter and mortal will with Spirit. And because this dualism, this contaminated conception, embraces no thought of Spirit's allness, it must inevitably be swallowed up by evil's claim to be all.

For human consciousness to begin to achieve the seamlessness—the unity and peace—that represents divine oneness, we must embrace the truth of God's allness taught by Christian Science. It is the pure idea of the allness of *Spirit,* good, that destroys conflict, and the fear of it, in the individual and in the universal thought and the whole body of mankind.

At this moment the world seems polarized as never before. Mankind is fearfully focused on the specter of total destruction. Terrorism, wars, addiction, the issues and diseases surrounding human sexuality, crime, separation in families, the abrogation of the legal and moral rights of all living beings—all of the symptoms of individual and collective conflict—constitute the carnal mind's denial of the oneness of real being. This is why the pure theology underlying the virgin birth is so essential, because as long as belief in matter's reality persists, there must be conflict. We can't naively continue to believe that the world is dealing merely with a conflict between human good and evil. We have seen that in the context of the belief of multiple causes, even the apparent good is inevitably polarized. Therefore, human goodness is not sufficient to redeem conflict. True redemption is, as promised, the task of the Saviour, the Christ, revealing the pure and infinite idea of Mind's allness and oneness.

The remarkable words opening "the scientific statement of being" in *Science and Health* kindle with new fire as we recognize more fully what they mean to the salvation of mankind. "There is no life, truth, intelligence, nor substance in matter," the words tell us. "All is infinite Mind and its infinite manifestation, for God is All-in-all" (*Science and Health*, p. 468).

And Jesus, knowing and proving that we are *all* the beloved sons and daughters of God, uttered the amazing words that to the end of time prophesy our demonstration of both spiritual origin and universal brotherhood. "Our Father which art in heaven," he prayed, "Hallowed be thy name" (Matt. 6:9).

—*Barbara Cook*

WHAT AM I SUPPOSED TO THINK ABOUT MY BODY?

*T*hrough my experience in the public practice of Christian Science, I've learned some fundamentals that I believe are indispensable for Christian Science treatment. For one thing, it's very important to establish the facts of spiritual reality right at the outset of treatment. Not just repeat the right words, but establish clearly in thought that man is wholly spiritual and not material. This calls for turning from fleshly appearances and contemplating instead what is true of man's identity as God's likeness. And what's true is that man reflects the limitless good that characterizes God's nature.

In *Science and Health with Key to the Scriptures,* Mary Baker Eddy, who discovered and founded Christian Science, explains, "The substance, Life, intelligence, Truth, and Love, which constitute Deity, are reflected by His creation; and when we subordinate the false testimony of the corporeal senses to the facts of Science, we shall see this true likeness and reflection everywhere" (p. 516).

If we believe that the condition of the physical body constitutes the actual state of a patient's health, our work will be protracted and even ineffective. *Science and Health* tells us, "A false sense of life, substance, and mind hides the divine possibilities, and conceals scientific demonstration" (pp. 325–326).

To my sense, when we give treatment in Christian Science, our starting point must be the scientific fact that man is spiritual, whole, and perfect now. Man is God's, Spirit's, reflection, and therefore can include only that which expresses God's own being. If it isn't in God, it can't be in His reflection. When you're convinced of this, only then do you have a solid basis for proving that man is not material and can never be a medium for disease or any other error.

But then the question may arise, "What am I supposed to think about my body? How can I believe I'm entirely spiritual, immortal, and perfect, when I see and feel this imperfect body every day? I feed it, dress it, care for it. It's the way everyone

identifies me. My body means a lot to me. I'm not ready to do without it even if I could."

So you might wonder, "What good does it do to insist, as Christian Science teaches, that man is entirely spiritual, not material?" Well, what good does it do to insist on the facts about the shape and rotation of the earth? It still looks as though the earth stands perfectly still and is relatively flat. But we know that the appearance is a deception. To be error-free—that is, undeceived—regarding the earth, we must hold to the scientific facts. That calls for turning from the physical sense evidence and acting instead upon what is known to be true. Great expansion of thought and discovery have followed a correct view of the earth.

We can reason similarly about man. The discovery of Christian Science has brought to light the astounding fact that man is actually the immortal reflection of God's own being. Then, he's not in a material body at all, because God is Spirit. Yes, it does look as if man is a mortal, living in a physical body. But if we believe that this appearance is factual, we're being deceived by a misconception. And a whole multitude of problems grows out of that mortal outlook. But it has been abundantly proved that to the degree we accept the revealed spiritual facts of man, we're able to demonstrate the limitless possibilities of freedom from bodily complaints.

We don't need to do without the body at this stage. We don't even want to do that. But we certainly do want to overcome the discords so frequently manifested in the body; and it is definitely right to do so. Our task is to learn how to exercise dominion over the body, and not let it dominate us. As *Science and Health* explains, "In proportion as matter loses to human sense all entity as man, in that proportion does man become its master" (p. 369).

One thing must be clear. The physical body is not the real man. Matter can never be the medium for man's true being. The body is an externalization of mortal concepts. And these concepts are all too frequently limiting because of ignorance of the spiritual reality.

When we declare that the body is not the true identity of man, and that man is wholly spiritual, we do so to establish in our thought a right sense of what is real. The man of God's creating is always healthy, concordant in every action. He is held forever in a perfect state, free from discords of every kind. We can prove this through spiritual understanding, prove that diseases and discords in the body represent false concepts, mental errors about man's true status and possibilities.

If matter is not the medium for man, why should we care about the condition of the body? Because the body displays much of our present sense of identity. And we want the body to be in conformity with the operation of the orderly and harmonious divine Principle that governs man.

This illustration might help. Think about an electronic calculator. It serves us usefully in making mathematical calculations. When using it, we expect the answer displayed on the calculator's screen to be consistent with mathematical laws. And it will be if our input into the calculator is correct.

But if we feed in the wrong information, the displayed answer won't be correct. For example, if you want to know the product of 9×17, but by mistake you insert 9×178, you'll get a wrong answer. Presumably you would know enough to tell at a glance that it's not correct. However, if you believed the displayed answer was accurate, and acted upon it as though it were true, you'd suffer the consequences. Not because the calculator had power to impose its mistake on you, but because you were deceived into believing a misconception.

You can draw similar conclusions about the body. The body isn't man; but it displays what we believe is true of man. Like the calculator, it's capable of displaying either correct or wrong "answers." If you hold your thought firmly to what you know are the scientific facts of man in God's likeness, the body will display conditions that are consistent with these facts. Thus the displayed "answer" will be in accord with the divine Principle that governs man's real being. But if, instead, you entertain erroneous beliefs about man, you shouldn't be surprised when the body displays conditions that couldn't be true of God's reflection.

As *Science and Health* explains: "A material body only expresses a material and mortal mind. . . . You embrace your body in your thought, and you should delineate upon it thoughts of health, not of sickness. You should banish all thoughts of disease and sin and of other beliefs included in matter" (pp. 208–209).

That's why it's so important to know that man is God's immortal idea, entirely spiritual, not material. God's idea is maintained forever as His perfect likeness. That immortal idea, man, has never been transformed into a material being. He cannot be made to embody the characteristics of mortality. Under God's government, man is always healthy, harmonious, functioning in perfect order. These are the effects of the operation of the producing, governing divine Principle—God. And this is the truth we need to realize in order to establish our well-being on a sure basis.

What happens when the body is discordant? The so-called mortal, carnal mind is speaking. Its basic, erroneous claim is that man is separate from God; and that his life, substance, and intelligence are embodied in matter. On that false premise it asserts that there's a cause operating in man that produces discord, and that the bodily inharmony is proof of its effect.

Only when we believe in the misconception—take in as true what the body is telling us—can we suffer any consequences. To be free of the error, we must do what would be done to correct an erroneous display on the screen of a calculator. We must correct the input that produced the wrong answer.

How do we do that? By refusing to give reality to that which is not spiritually true of man. In truth, God holds man in perfect unity with Himself and manifests His immutable perfection through His reflection, man. When the bodily appearance fails to conform to this scientific fact, it's not the body that needs correction. The discord in the body is an externalization of mortal thought. To remove what's externalized, human consciousness must be correctly instructed by what is true according to God's revelation of divine Science. When errors of belief are corrected through spiritual understanding, this has a corrective effect on the body.

Science and Health states: "The understanding that the Ego is Mind, and that there is but one Mind or intelligence, begins at once to destroy the errors of mortal sense and to supply the truth of immortal sense. This understanding makes the body harmonious; it makes the nerves, bones, brain, etc., servants, instead of masters. If man is governed by the law of divine Mind, his body is in submission to everlasting Life and Truth and Love" (p. 216).

Isn't it apparent, then, that to make the body harmonious we must uplift consciousness by yielding thought to the truth of immortal being; by realizing that now and always man is the perfect expression of infinite Mind? Divine Mind is forever expressing its own infinite being in man. That means man's life, substance, intelligence, his consciousness and individuality, are entirely spiritual, expressing the perfection of Mind.

This is true right now, today. None of the contrary conceptions that appear real to the mortal senses can change or interfere with that reality. And all the false beliefs universally accepted about man can never separate us from the ability to prove that God's loving, unfailing support is always present to save us from such errors. As the Apostle Paul wrote: "Who shall separate us from the love of Christ? shall tribulation, or distress, or persecution, or famine, or nakedness, or peril, or sword? . . . Nay, in all these things we are more than conquerors through him that loved us." And then he goes on to say that nothing "shall be able to separate us from the love of God, which is in Christ Jesus our Lord" (Rom. 8:35, 37, 39).

This truth of man's inseparability from God was central to Jesus' marvelous healing works. He knew that divine Mind, God, holds man intact in a perfect state, and that nothing can separate him from God's government. Someone's body might have indicated that man was crippled, or blind, or even dead. But Jesus knew such conditions were lies—errors of thought—that could never be identified with the scientific reality of man. In the case of the man with the withered hand, Mrs. Eddy says of Jesus, "He heeded not the taunt, 'That withered hand looks very real and feels very real;' but he cut off this vain boasting and destroyed human pride by taking away the material evidence" (*Unity of Good*, p. 11).

We can do the same. Instead of looking at man simply as a physical body, we're equipped to discern his identity the way the Science of being reveals him to be. As the truth of man and of Mind's perfect government acts upon human consciousness, this truth transforms thought, and the error is relinquished. When that happens, the error can no longer be manifested in the body—the patient is healed.

If we're going to make progress in exercising dominion over the body, the primary question to be considered is, What acts as cause in man? The answer is, It is not the body and it is not mortal mind. *Science and Health* says: "Divine Mind is the only cause or Principle of existence. Cause does not exist in matter, in mortal mind, or in physical forms" (p. 262).

That's a vital point in Christian Science treatment. We must affirm the fact that God, divine Principle, is the only cause. And then know, really be convinced, that man is a living manifestation of the order and harmony forever expressed through the government of divine Principle.

When we recognize that bodily inharmony represents an error of belief that cannot possibly be true of what God makes manifest in man, we have a scientific basis for expelling the error of belief. And that's done as we understand that matter is never the substance of man. Instead, man is entirely spiritual and is governed only by the laws of God, Spirit.

—*David E. Sleeper*

"WHO SHALL BE GREATEST?"

*H*ave you ever noticed how most little children play together harmoniously in a sandbox or schoolyard, but sometimes there's a kid who tries to grab all the toys or bully others? There may be many opinions about where this tendency comes from, but most of us would agree it has some connection with a desire to be first. The king of the mountain. The discoverer of Christian Science, Mary Baker Eddy, observed, "Two personal queries give point to human action: Who shall be greatest? and, Who shall be best?" (*Miscellaneous Writings 1883-1896*, p. 268).

This trait may start in childhood games, but in one form or another, it appears in the thought of most of us as we mature. Just the other day an outstanding major league baseball player said he used performance-enhancing drugs because he wanted to be the best ballplayer in the world.

The desire to be greatest is not new, of course. At least once, Jesus' disciples argued over who was the greatest among them (see Mark 9:33, 34). And the mother of two of them once asked Jesus to give them a favored place with him (see Matt. 20:20, 21).

Competitive conflicts may be academic and even cordial at the entry level. But they don't always stay that way. There is an ascending scale of intensity and the competition can become unpleasant as deeper assumptions are being challenged. Many earnest thinkers, such as some in the medical, theological, and scientific fields, feel that the future of their personal reputations is at stake when positions they hold or discoveries they have perhaps spent their lives studying, are challenged. They strongly desire to be best or greatest with ideas, theories, discoveries, teaching, authorship, institutional founding and funding, etc. Mrs. Eddy observed, "Competition in commerce, deceit in councils, dishonor in nations, dishonesty in trusts, begin with 'Who shall be greatest?'" (*Message to The Mother Church for 1902*, p. 4).

At some point in this ascending scale of competition, selfish desires can drive people to use harmful mental means to gain their ends. Sandbox problems can intensify into what Mrs. Eddy referred to as animal magnetism and mental malpractice. Those are the use of hostile and often harsh mental practices to establish one's superiority. Mrs. Eddy observed: "The mild forms of animal magnetism are disappearing, and its aggressive features are coming to the front. The looms of crime, hidden in the dark recesses of mortal thought, are every hour weaving webs more complicated and subtle" (*Science and Health*, p. 102).

Mrs. Eddy knew whereof she wrote. But she was not an eager investigator of subtle evil intrigue. Probably none of us is. It is like exploring a dimly lighted cavern inhabited by poisonous serpents. She wrote: "I shall not forget the cost of investigating, for this age, the methods and power of error. While the ways, means, and potency of Truth had flowed into my consciousness as easily as dawns the morning light and shadows flee, the metaphysical mystery of error—its hidden paths, purpose, and fruits—at first defied me. I was saying all the time, 'Come not thou into the secret'—but at length took up the research according to God's command" (*Miscellaneous Writings 1883-1896*, pp. 222–223).

There are many examples of her experience with this evil mental influence to which others were, and even today still are, so blind that they ridiculed Mrs. Eddy then and Christian Scientists today for discussing it.

For instance, there are problems within Church experience. On page 44 of *Retrospection and Introspection*, Mrs. Eddy described in detail what happened with her Church in Boston at one period, and how she solved the problem. Briefly, while she was in charge, the Church prospered. When she was called by God to other duties and stopped preaching every Sunday, the members couldn't sustain the progress and harmony. As she analyzed the situation, she realized the crisis had arisen because the members failed to take the time and make the effort to protect their thoughts from opposing mental elements she herself had recognized and neutralized through prayer. They quarreled with one another under its hidden influence. They were unaware of what she saw clearly as, ". . . the envy and molestation of other churches, and . . . the danger to its members which must always lie in Christian warfare."

She recommended the Church dissolve. Apparently that was enough to either awake the members or distract their enemies, or both, because a degree of harmony and prosperity were restored. The Church was reorganized a few years later on a more spiritual basis that endured.

This 1890s situation has a parallel today. Though Christian Science has gained important and appropriate recognition in some sectors of public thought, a brief glance at Internet postings shows it is still bitterly, openly opposed in other sectors.

A basic reason for opposition could be a struggle over the question, Who shall be greatest, matter or Spirit, God? The world of organized mortal belief insists that all reality originates in and is wholly controlled by the so-called laws of matter. It insists that the rise, condition of existence, and fall of all things are controlled by those laws, which cannot be modified or altered any more than the sunrise or seasons can be changed.

On the other hand, the theology of Christian Science reveals that all reality is created and sustained by God, divine Mind. It reveals the allness of the one God, and man as His perfect expression, forever at one with Him. It proves through practical and undeniable healing that what is called evil in any form is a belief or error that can, and even certainly will, be dissolved by God's Christ, or His loving embrace of His creation.

This truth is the gentle, powerful Comforter Christ Jesus promised. It is the final revelation of scientific, spiritual healing, in the broadest application of that word. It is the hope of the age because it is saving the race from aggressive, organized efforts to force humanity to accept the lie that matter, not God, is supreme. This aggression may be the ultimate sandbox problem. God, not matter, is the greatest. The superiority of God proves the nothingness of matter. The laws of God prove the falsity of the so-called laws of matter.

Given the nature of opposition in Christ Jesus' day and in Mrs. Eddy's life, it should not be surprising that her Church today would experience challenges.

Some say these challenges are natural cycles of human events and organizations, like cycles in the stock market. Others feel the theology of Christian Science has been largely superseded by progress in material medicine, although the general public is abandoning matter-based medicine in search of methods with better healing records, including the system of Christian Science. Some observers hold the view that Christian Science is simply being challenged as the years pass since its Founder was active. And there are suggestions that some internal decisions over the past century have harmed it.

As reasonable as these explanations are from human perspectives, it seems fair to ask if they reach the level of moral and spiritual insight Mrs. Eddy had to attain to solve similar problems in her early Church. She saw that church challenges can arise from unhandled, hidden, subtle, and sometimes malicious mental influences. For instance, are there unnatural inclinations in the thoughts and characters of members that are ripe for removal because they undermine the holiness from which sweet spiritual healing unfolds? Does a gentle sense of compromise and brotherly love permeate members' thoughts, or do they demand to have their own opinions heard in an effort to be greatest? Do kindness, good will, and Christian appreciation set the tone of private conversations about one another, or do personal comments and criticism creep in?

It is helpful in defeating evil to not mistake outward or secondary effects for primary, hidden causes. To be alert to the secret, malicious purpose of mental opposition helps anyone understand that inharmony, strife, etc., are the secondary level of evil's seeming operation. The primary level is the malice and envy inherent in what Paul referred to as the carnal mind and Mrs. Eddy referred to as mortal mind. This basic evil manifests itself in those systems that would be greatest and that would take any steps to achieve that end. Mrs. Eddy explained candidly, "The powers of evil are leagued together in secret conspiracy against the Lord and against His Christ, as expressed and operative in Christian Science." She also said that "large numbers" are "organizing action against us" (*Mis.*, p. 177). She explained: "The natural fruits of Christian Science Mind-healing are harmony, brotherly love, spiritual growth and activity. The malicious aim of perverted mind-power, or animal magnetism, is to paralyze good and give activity to evil. It starts factions and engenders envy and hatred . . ." (*The First Church of Christ, Scientist, and Miscellany*, p. 213). This often subtle, malicious action is discussed in detail in the Bible book of Apocalypse (Revelation), and in the *Science and Health* chapter with the same name.

To the great relief of humanity, Mrs. Eddy also discovered that every phase of evil, no matter how intricate or subtle, is powerless before God, divine Love. She wrote, "Evil is not supreme; good is not helpless; nor are the so-called laws of matter primary, and the law of Spirit secondary" (*Science and Health*, p. 207). Her early experience indicates the members were simply less attentive to earnest study than they needed to be in order to uncover and nullify the bold and malicious mental elements that would undermine their best efforts and deprive the whole human family of the one system of healing that saves from all evil. As they let the Christ awaken them to pray consistently about the nothingness of unseen, secret, mental opposition, their Church and its members were roused to fulfill their healing mission for the world. Those healing gifts did not diminish, but they naturally expanded and prospered in right ways. As we are alert and obedient today, the same result is assured. God is the one, great I AM.

—*J. Thomas Black*

THE YOUTH-AND-MORALITY ARTICLE

⸎

*T*he Editors of the *Journal* asked me to write this. I cast about aimlessly for a while, thinking only of articles on youth and morality I *didn't* want to write. Like the "stern-and-scolding" one. Or the "I-told-you-so" one. Or the "Wow!-haven't-standards-dropped-into-the-basement" one. On the other hand, I also wasn't interested in writing a "Let's-be-open-minded-about-anything-anyone-does" article.

Then a passage surfaced, so profound in its meaning that it practically invites the thinker in for deeper contemplation. It is from the Christian Science textbook, *Science and Health with Key to the Scriptures* by Mary Baker Eddy: "Higher enjoyments alone can satisfy the cravings of immortal man" (pp. 60–61). The last few words caught my attention first: "the cravings of immortal man." I knew from study of the Bible that immortal man is the flawless and sinless expression of God. God created man in His own likeness, complete in every way, including all good, lacking nothing. So what is there for immortal man to *crave?*

As I pondered this, I took a closer look at my concept of immortal man. Oh, I used appropriate, metaphysically accurate words whenever speaking or writing on the subject. But something about my concept of man didn't feel quite right. I hadn't been considering God's man as dynamic. And yet the man that craves isn't static at all! I began to see something alive and powerful about man's true nature. It's a mistake to think our choice is between being a bland individual who does not crave and a vital one who sometimes craves evil. The real man, your true identity, is boundlessly vital and craves good.

Research in the Bible and in Mrs. Eddy's writings uncovers concepts closely related to craving. For instance, Christ Jesus speaks of hungering and thirsting. Mrs. Eddy speaks of heartfelt desire and affection. Notice, if you do this research, that the reader isn't being asked to get rid of the affections, to stomp on right desire, to shut off the hungering, or deny the craving for good. In fact, quite the opposite is advised.

For instance, a passage in *Science and Health* reads, "Desire is prayer; and no loss can occur from trusting God with our desires, that they may be moulded and exalted before they take form in words and in deeds" (p. 1). We're encouraged not to get rid of the affections but to let them be enriched (see Mary Baker Eddy, *Manual of The Mother Church*, Art. VIII, Sect. 4). We're to have a hungering and thirsting for righteousness—and it will be filled (see Matt. 5:6). These ideas, which I'd found in my studying, were wonderfully encouraging. Desire is really prayer. Craving in its truest sense is spiritual yearning.

The desire to be somebody, to live a life that shines and shows forth artistic brilliance, for instance, or athletic excellence, is wonderful. The hungering to love and to be loved is natural and deserves nourishment. The craving we each have to be the full and fulfilled expression of God is a true and right craving. The spiritual truth of man's being is seen humanly in a natural yearning for good things in our daily lives.

Yet while strong desires and cravings are not necessarily wrong, there is something very wrong with the carnal mind's claim that it can satisfy our cravings. It cannot.

The *carnal mind*—a Bible term—refers to a totally selfish and depraved mentality, but also a totally false one. The basic view of this so-called mind is that life is physical, godless, and ultimately without meaning. Starting from that wrongheaded premise, the carnal mind leads to wrong conclusions, shipwrecking honest desire in the process.

The carnal mind would try to twist a craving downward—away from what is natural and good and wholesome—into something perverse. For example, the desire to excel at whatever we do is good. But it is the carnal mind trying to twist that desire downward when we want to excel at slaughtering the enemy in an extremely violent video game or in a street gang. The longing to defeat loneliness and be in close contact with friends is great. It's only carnal mind "solutions" for that longing that would drag one into foolish things like an obsession with food or experimentation with drugs in the hope of gaining social acceptance.

Emptiness. That's the typical inclination of the carnal mind: toward darkness, toward selfishness, away from positive achievement. This is never, however, the natural inclination of man, of you or me! It's normal for each of us to have a deep yearning, a hungering and a thirsting, for what is truly good. It's natural for each of us to crave the love that comes from divine Love.

Once we have glimpsed, though, that the problem is not appropriate desires or cravings, but rather the carnal mind's lying claim that *it* can satisfy those desires, our needed response is to defeat the false claim without defeating the craving!

Morality—the code for human behavior that helps keep us on track, steering us away from harmful influences—has more than a human basis. Actually, moral law didn't spring from human society but from the divine presence. When Moses went up Mount Sinai to receive the Ten Commandments, he didn't meet with the Student Ethics Committee! What he came back down with was not a document born of debate and consensus. The moral law given by God does good for you and me. The purpose of moral law is not to keep good times away from us but to show us what those good times really are and to provide the right context in which to experience them.

Some things become obsolete. Some things never do. In school I had a professor who said live theater was obsolete and should be considered dead. Then a friend pointed out that people have been pronouncing the theater dead for at least four thousand years. Moral law is a bit like that. People have been calling it outmoded ever since Moses came down the mountain. But it still serves as a needed causeway whereon one can safely travel, and whereon one can yearn and desire for good and see that craving come to fulfillment. It's beyond the grasp of the carnal mind. Moral law is the road, though not the destination. True craving is what keeps us moving along the road.

God, the power that creates man and governs the universe, is pure Mind, wholly good. The divine Mind is the exact opposite of the carnal mind, and it is the only real Mind, the only genuine power or source of thought. God, divine Mind, is the impeller of our true desires and yearnings and cravings. God is also our most faithful friend. What we yearn to become, what we in truth already are—these are found in Mind, in Love. The Mind that made man is the Mind that knows man as its pure spiritual likeness, that animates man and enlivens him. It's the Mind that forever satisfies and fulfills man and that maintains his completeness and well-being.

Our part is to claim this Mind as the only true consciousness, our consciousness. It is to live as if this were true and to *know* that it is true—because it *is*. Then we stay above the swamp of the carnal mentality. We find what a dynamic thing it is to be the man God made, the man that craves good.

—*Channing Walker*

INDEXES

Partial Subject Index

Partial Subject Index

Partial Subject Index

PARTIAL SUBJECT INDEX

Partial Subject Index

Partial Subject Index

Partial Subject Index

Author Index

Author Index

Publication Date Index

PUBLICATION DATE INDEX

NOTES

Notes

NOTES

NOTES

NOTES

ABOUT MARY BAKER EDDY

*M*ary Baker Eddy, the Discoverer and Founder of Christian Science, was healed of life-threatening injuries by praying and reading her Bible, including the account in the Gospel of Mark about Christ Jesus healing a man of palsy. Following her healing, she committed her life to understanding how Jesus healed. She explained her discovery of Christian Science in her book called *Science and Health with Key to the Scriptures*, which was published in 1875. This book has opened the inspired meaning of the Bible to millions. To help spread this message of healing, Mrs. Eddy founded the Church of Christ, Scientist, in 1879 "…to commemorate the word and works of our Master, which should reinstate primitive Christianity and its lost element of healing" (*Manual of The Mother Church*, p. 17). She began publishing magazines and eventually a newspaper, to enable the Christ-message to reach a wider audience.

For more information about Mary Baker Eddy, please visit
www.marybakereddylibrary.org